Cider

Cider

Photography by Mark Bolton

Contributing authors

Jonathan Briggs
Ted Bruning
Richard Cheshire
Sue Clifford
Alan Golding
Angela King
Dave Matthews

Henry May
Tom Oliver
Michael Pooley
Simon Russell
Adrian Tierney-Jones
Gillian Williams

Published by the Campaign for Real Ale Ltd
230 Hatfield Road
St Albans
Hertfordshire AL1 1LA
www.camra.org.uk/books

ISBN 978-1-85249-259-5

A CIP catalogue record for this book is available from
the British Library.

Printed and bound in Singapore by KHL Printing Co Pte Ltd

Managing Editor: Simon Hall
Project Editor: Katie Hunt
Editorial Assistance: Emma Haines
Design/Typography: Linda Storey (Top Floor Design Ltd)
Photography: Mark Bolton
Maps: John Plumer (JP Map Graphics Ltd)
Indexer: Hilary Bird
Marketing Manager: Kim Carvey

Picture credits
The publisher would like to thank the contributors and
institutions who have kindly given permission for their
photography to be published in this publication. Special
thanks go to **Mark Bolton** for his excellent commissioned
photography, and to the many cider and perry
organisations around the country who assisted him.

Specific thanks go to: p13 (below) **NACM**, p14 **NACM**,
p16 **NACM**, p17 **NACM**, p22 **NACM**, p26 (below)
Gwynt y Ddraig, p27 (below) **Gwynt y Ddraig**, p86
L. Storey, p87 **L. Storey**, p98 **NACM**, p99 **CAMRA
archive**, p100 **CAMRA archive**, p106 **CAMRA archive**,
p107 **CAMRA archive**, p108 **CAMRA archive**, p109
G. Williams, p135 **D. Matthews**, p137 **D. Matthews**,
p138 (above) **D. Matthews**, (below) **J M. Osoro**, p139
D. Matthews, p140 **D. Matthews**, p141 **J M. Osoro**, p142
D. Matthews, p143 **D. Matthews**, p144 **D. Matthews**,
p145 **D. Matthews**, p146 **D. Matthews**, p147 **D.
Matthews**, p148 **D. Matthews**, p149 **D. Matthews**,
p150 **D. Matthews**, p151 **Mostviertel Tourismus,
Austria/www.weinfranz.at**, p152 **Mostviertel
Tourismus, Austria/www.weinfranz.at**, p153
Mostviertel Tourismus, Austria/www.weinfranz.at,
p154 **A. Golding**, p155 (above) **A. Golding**, (below)
Mostviertel Tourismus, Austria/www.weinfranz.at,
p156 **A. Golding**, p157 **Mostviertel Tourismus,
Austria/www.weinfranz.at**, p158 **A. Golding**,
p159 **A. Golding**, p160 **A. Golding**, p161 **A. Golding**,
p162 **A. Golding**, p163 **A. Golding**, p164 **A. Golding**,
p165 **Domaine Pinnacle**

Front cover: Top (L-R) **Ross on Wye Cider and Perry**,
M. Bolton (Olivers Cider and Perry), **M. Bolton**
(Minchew's Real Cyder & Perry); Second line (L-R) **M.
Bolton** (Bonython Estate Gardens), **M. Bolton** (Hecks
Farmhouse Cider), **M. Bolton** (Burrow Hill Cider);
Third line (L-R) **M. Bolton** (Burrow Hill Cider), **M.
Bolton**, **M. Bolton** (Burrow Hill Cider); Bottom (L-R)
G. Hall, **M. Bolton** (Perry Brothers), **M. Bolton**
(Bonython Estate Gardens); Back cover: **M. Bolton**
(Thatchers Cider); Front flap: **M. Bolton**

Thanks also to the Old Scrump's Cider House website
www.ciderandperry.co.uk for their help in compiling the
chapters on the history of cider and perry.

Contents

The Authors

Adrian Tierney-Jones

Ted Bruning

Michael Pooley

NACM

Gillian Williams

Dave Matthews

Adrian Tierney-Jones is an Exmoor-based award-winning journalist who specialises in writing about drink and rural life. The first cider he drank was Strongbow, but he's better now. Current favourites include ciders from Dunkerton, Gwynt y Ddraig, Gwatkin and Westons. He used to live on the Somerset Levels, next door to an old farmer who regularly made his own cider; this sparked an interest in the whole West Country cider culture. He's also a massive fan of perry, considering it to be a greatly under-appreciated drink.

Ted Bruning was editor of CAMRA's newspaper *What's Brewing* from 1999-2006. He also edited *What's Brewing*'s quarterly supplement, 'Cider Press', from 1996-2000, and the 1995 edition of CAMRA's *Good Cider Guide*. Other books include *Historic Pubs of London*, *Historic Inns of England*, *The Microbrewers' Handbook* and *London By Pub*.

Michael Pooley has been making cider and studying the craft since 1978 when he moved to Shropshire and inherited several apple trees. He set up the Shropshire Apple Trust in 1999, an organisation which promotes apple culture in all its guises. His cidermaking courses have acquired a national reputation, and he has written extensively on the subject, including the highly successful standard text *Real Cidermaking on a Small Scale*.

Simon Russell is the spokesperson for the National Association of Cider Makers (NACM). Founded in 1920, the NACM promotes the UK cider and perry industry. It represents both the larger producers and the many hundreds of smaller scale cider makers. The NACM is engaged with government and a range of agencies to ensure that the interests of cider makers, fruit growers and consumers are considered and well represented.

Gillian Williams has been involved with CAMRA's cider and perry committee for over 10 years, holding the positions of Secretary, Chair and, for 4 years, National Director of Cider & Perry. Her guiding principles are quality, passion, involvement and knowledge. Gill has judged at championship level and trained others.

Dave Matthews wrote his first cider article for CAMRA's *What's Brewing* in 1998, going on to edit CAMRA's *Good Cider Guide* in 2000. Also in 2000, he founded his cider company, Seidr Dai, in Cardiff. Seidr Dai specialises in producing ciders and perries from rare and endangered Welsh varieties. In 2001, Alan Golding and Dave founded the Welsh Perry and Cider Society, whose annual festival and championships have helped to raise the number of Welsh cidermakers from five to over thirty.

Thank you to José María Osoro, President of the Asturian Cidermakers Association, for his help and proof reading of the Spanish section. Thanks too to French cidermaker Adam Bland for his help with the French section.

Alan Golding

Sue & Angela

Common Ground

Tom Oliver

Henry May

Jonathan Briggs

Alan Golding trained his palate while working as assistant manager of a wine merchant and co-founded the Welsh Perry and Cider Society in 2001, while working in radio and television production. In 2007 he was hired by the Society on a consultancy basis made possible by funding from the Welsh Assembly Government. He is on a mission to bring the cider and perry producing regions of the world to the attention of the British public.

Sue Clifford & **Angela King** are the founder directors of Common Ground and have been pioneering for orchards and local distinctiveness for over two decades. Their recent books include *England in Particular: A celebration of the commonplace, the local, the vernacular and the distinctive*; *The Apple Source Book* – a guide to enriching both our culinary and cultural landscapes – and the *Community Orchard Handbook*.

Tom Oliver is a cider and perry maker from Ocle Pychard in Herefordshire. He was drinking before he began producing and then started selling in 1999. 'I take what the fruit gives me' says Tom, 'so every year throws up a unique vintage. I believe that Slow Food's Three Counties Perry Presidium is a great stepping stone for perry and progressive perry producers'.

Henry May was once the (Customs &) Excise Officer for Herefordshire, whose responsibilities included the policing of cider duty. His conversion from gamekeeper to poacher has included the collection and protection from extinction of cider apple varieties in thirty acres of orchards in England at Tidnor Wood (www.tidnorwood.org.uk), and a similar venture in France.

Jonathan Briggs has worked in nature conservation for over 25 years. He ran the Plantlife/BSBI National Mistletoe Survey in the 1990s, and has been involved in many mistletoe conservation and management projects since – now running the Mistletoe Matters Consultancy. He has a particular interest in the mistletoe trade around Tenbury Wells, Worcestershire.

Mark Bolton is a freelance photographer specialising in lifestyle, gardens, interiors and country matters, and is also a keen cider maker and drinker. Married with two children, he lives in Bristol but travels widely and is currently finishing photography for the book *Go Slow Italy*.

Thanks go to all the cider makers and orchard owners who gave me access to their properties, and in many cases allowed me to photograph at very early or very busy times of the day. Special thanks to Julian Temperley at Burrow Hill, and Rob Uren of Malvern Magic who pointed me in the right direction and have been especially helpful in trying to understand this ancient art of cider making. I'd also like to thank Roger Wilkins, Gwatkin's Cider, Perry's Cider, Heck's Farmhouse Cider, Sheppy's Cider, Upton's Cider, Gray's Cider, Newton's Cider, Oliver's Cider and Perry, Ross On Wye Cider, Brimblecombe's Cider, John Thatcher, Martin Latimer and Kevin Minchew for taking time out of their busy schedules.

Introduction

**The impressive cider range
at Ye Olde Cider Bar**

Introduction

Newton Abbot is an unremarkable Devon town, overshadowed by its
raffishly glamorous seaside neighbour Torquay to the south, and the
granite playground of Dartmoor to the north. However, while Torquay
and the English Riviera have sun, sand and sea, and Dartmoor a touch
of the wilderness, Newton Abbot has a unique attraction that earns it a
mention in this book: its cider house – Ye Olde Cider Bar.

Stepping into this venerable establishment is like taking a trip back in
time. Outside, the main road is crammed with speeding traffic, inside it's
another world: the furniture is off-the-peg fittings from the 1970s; the floor
is uncompromising stone; unfashionable creams and browns swirl about
on the walls; jugs and tankards hang over the bar. However, it's what is
behind the counter that anchors the bar within another time and place: this
is one of the few remaining cider-only establishments left in the country.

There's no ale here, just ciders, perries and fruit wines. Four massive
40-gallon barrels dispense ciders from local producer Winkleigh, while
smaller pins offer ciders and perries from the likes of Thatchers and
Westons. There are also bottles of single-varietal ciders plus taps to
dispense chilled draught ciders. Cider might be the fashionable drink of
the past few years, but be warned: ask for cider over ice and the owner
will show you the door...

Cider has its home in the town here, but its heart is in the countryside. Think cider and it's difficult to escape its rural origins. Beer also begins in a field of barley, but brewing is indisputably industrial – whether long-standing regional brewer or one man and a mash tun. Beers may be sold as hand-crafted but the reality in the majority of cases is a stainless steel, computer-run operation. Cider, on the other hand, still doggedly holds onto its rural connections.

Take a golden glass of cider, sprightly and gloriously sharp, and one sip can conjure up a scene of autumn mists strolling lazily over gently sloping fields, stroking the ancient hedgerows and trees; meanwhile beams of shy sunlight break through the pall, casting a pale light on orchards laden with ripe fruit. Another sip and it's harvest time as cider apples are gathered in. A musty, earthy, softly sweet aroma fills the air around the timber-framed barns of the cider-making farms. This is a bucolic scene repeated up and down country lanes in the prime cider-producing areas of England: Herefordshire, the neighbouring counties of Worcestershire and Gloucestershire, and further afield in Somerset, Devon, Kent, Norfolk and Suffolk. Even Wales gets a look-in these days as the success of Ralph's and Gwynt y Ddraig can testify.

Despite the appeal of this Sylvan flight of imagination, the best-selling ciders are more likely to be associated with lorries loaded with apples and massive conveyor belts heavy with fruit snaking through a warehouse-like space. All too often concentrate is used. Meanwhile, their publicity departments take aim at drinkers with edgy prose and the latest gimmicks: ice cubes in the glass, near-frozen cider and speciality flavours that should stay in the fruit bowl.

However, it's the artisanal cidermakers, not the industrial producers, that this book is concerned with: whether long-established family firms such as Aspall and Westons, or more recent arrivals like Dunkertons and Gwatkin. These are the heroes of cider.

Cider (and to a lesser extent its close cousin perry) has shaped parts of our native landscape since time immemorial. The Celts were apparently the first to realise that the fermented juice of apples provided the basis for a damn good booze-up. Then the Romans came with their wine and the grape's eternal striving to be top dog has continued ever since. Long after the Roman Empire had shifted eastwards to Constantinople, the Normans imported their love of cider to these islands. It's not for nothing that Normandy to this day remains one of the most important cider regions in Europe.

In the Middle Ages such was the popularity of cider that the church forbid its use in the baptism font. In the tumultuous years of the 17th century, when they weren't fighting each other, gentlemen regarded Redstreak cider to be as refined and elegant as the finest wines of France. According to cider historian James Crowden, 'The heyday of cider was in the 1650s onwards when it was popular due to the lack of imported wine. After that, it became sandwiched between beer and wine.'

Samuel Pepys wrote about drinking a 'cup of syder', while Thomas Hardy rhapsodised 'sweet cyder is a great thing, a great thing to me'. Until recently traditional cider was the preferred drink in the rural (and not so rural) areas of the West Country. Farmers used to attract workers by the quality of their cider. Many still remember the days when men on the harvest used to drink a gallon of cider every day. Each. Stone jugs were placed at each end of the field to encourage them to work faster.

'Whenever you called at someone's farm,' one retired Somerset farmer once told me, 'the first thing they would ask is whether you wanted some cider. And of course the quality was important. Farm workers would move onto other places if the quality wasn't good.' Old hands at the game also knew to put the stopper back in the jug, otherwise slugs would crawl into the liquid and the next person to take a gulp would get more than they bargained for.

There was another reason for cider's popularity in Somerset. The county once had a strong Methodist tradition and chapel folk didn't want to be seen lurching out of the pub, so they made their drinks at home. One cider maker told me that when he was starting out, a veteran advised him that a lot of his best customers were teetotallers in name only!

What is cider? Simply put, it's the fermented juice of the apple, though not any old apple. Cider making is not rocket science but it does need finesse and a sense of what the end result will be.

First, catch your apples. However, forget supermarket favourites such as Granny Smith and Golden Delicious – cider apples have gloriously evocative names such as Sweet Alford, Tremlett's Bitter, Kingston Black and the aforementioned Redstreak. These are names inspired by the fruit's place of origin or the first person to cultivate them (though you've got to wonder who brought Slack-ma-girdle into the world). They also have more in common with the bullet-like, unpalatable crab apple than anything found in the supermarket. If you bite into one of the cider apples that West Country and Three Counties producers use, chances are your mouth would go on strike, such would be the harsh tannic attack.

In these regions apples have been grown for their suitability for cider for at least 400 years. They are chosen for their levels of tannins, acids and sweetness: sweet, bittersweet, sharp and bittersharp. Further east, in East Anglia and Kent, dessert apples are blended with cider apples, which helps to balance the underlying sweetness. Apples harvested early on in the season are the ones with the tannins and acids, while later ones are sweeter. The trick is to get the right blend of apples, which means that each cidermaker has their own unique mix.

After collection from the orchard – usually a laborious process involving long ash poles to knock down the fruit – the apples are crushed in a mill and the pulp is layered between steel plates in a cider press. Traditionally, this 'cheese' was layered between hessian sackcloths, but steel plates are now more commonly used. After the press is brought down several times, the pure apple juice is collected and left to ferment with added yeast. Some makers, replicating the methods of the lambic producers of Belgium, prefer to let wild yeasts play a role.

In the Middle Ages such was the popularity of cider that the church forbid its use in the baptism font

The quality and taste depend on the apple variety and blend of apples used. A few weeks after the long slumber of fermentation, a cider flexing its muscles at an alcoholic strength of between 6-8% abv is available. Some ciders are left to mature in oak barrels where they become stronger and drier. The legendary and popular cider style known as farmhouse scrumpy is made when yeast in the bottle continues the process of conditioning, producing a muscular, full-bodied cider. Scrumpy is invariably strong and usually still, with the character of wine.

Just like beer, cider has its different flavours and categories. Dry cider is traditionally associated with Somerset (some say Devon ciders can be sweeter, others dismiss such easy categorisation). Dry means that the cider should possess a mouth-drying astringency plus a crisp bite on the palate; the dryness can be mouth-puckering and often quite challenging, but the best examples of this style have a complexity and nobility that deserve reflection and contemplation. Medium cider has a more voluptuous and rounded figure and is less biting and tannic on the tongue. It is easy drinking and a crowd pleaser, though no less exalted. Sweet cider, as the name suggests, is a sweeter, more elegant creature, though still possessing a refreshing palate. Finally, there are specialist ciders – we are not talking industrial ciders with various blends of fruit juices added, or cider lite, an abomination that seems to be making its presence more and more felt – but something much more creative. These ciders are the apotheosis of the cidermaker's art: organic ciders, ciders made with apples from a single orchard and single varietal ciders.

Single varietal cider, where only one type of apple is used, is one of the most successful innovations of craft cidermakers in the last few years. (Though one cidermaker did say to me that he thought it like making cider with one hand behind your back – to him the skill of cider making is in the blend of different apples.) It has replicated the success of single-varietal wines and helped to lift the image of cider and even place it on the dining table. Sheppy's, an old family firm on the outskirts of Taunton, has become noted for its single-varietals. According to Louisa Sheppy, 'You need new ideas all the time and the single varietals have been a fantastic success. Without them I think we would have found things very hard. We battle against the negative image of cider all the time, which is why it's important for it to be progressive. Cider is a high quality drink.'

Her last sentence says it all: cider is a quality drink, a refreshing drink and a thirst-quencher, but it can also be a complex and diverse drink, a companion on the dining table and a link back to our country's rural past.

Then there is perry, cider's close cousin, the fermented juice of the perry pear – a complex, deliciously fruity-flavoured, light-coloured treat that drinks like a German or Alsatian white wine. It can be sparkling or still. It can be as light as a feather, delicate on the tongue, or singing with toffee, baked pear and even caramel notes. Its English heartland is Herefordshire, Worcestershire and Gloucestershire, though Welsh perries are starting to make an appearance, and Hecks of Somerset make one.

Perry was first mentioned back in the late 16th century when Elizabeth I granted the city of Worcester the right to incorporate three pears in its coat of arms. During the 'good old days', perry pears had fantastically evocative names such as Merrylegs, Mumblehead, Lumberskull and Devildrink. Today there are less than ten recognised perry varieties still grown – Huffcap is one of the favourites. Sadly, it's a rare beast of a beverage and rarely found in pubs, but if discovered it's thoroughly recommended.

Just like cask beer, craft cider making nearly died out as large-scale brands spent a fortune on TV advertising and produced bland and fizzy apple-tasting alcoholic drinks. Producers have fought back with well-crafted cider, and CAMRA has campaigned for traditionally-made, adjunct-free cider. Various initiatives have also taken place: October is Cider Month, there's also Cider Pub of the Year, the National Cider and Perry awards and the Pomona Award, a prestigious accolade that goes to a group, individual or business that works toward establishing real cider and perry as a premium product. Various CAMRA beer festivals also have ciders and perries for sale.

Cider and perry have a long and glorious history in this country and this lovingly-produced book proudly celebrates this sense of heritage. Long may it continue. Wassail!

> Cider is a quality drink, a refreshing drink and a thirst-quencher

The History of Cider

Apple growing in the UK

The Romans gave the Caucasus Mountains the forbidding title of 'end of all the Earth'. Cider lovers will no doubt have a more benign view of this region and its adjoining areas: this is the place where the main ancestors of the modern apple – *Malus pumila* and *Malus sylvestris* – emerged. Thanks to a natural hybridisation between these two fruits thousands of years ago, edible or non-sour apples developed and the long march to a cool glass of cider began.

The apple spread throughout the ancient world, travelling along the fertile crescent of the Middle East – Persia, the Caspian Sea, Palestine, Egypt and modern-day Turkey – an area that also saw the rise of farming and the development of beer. The earliest written account of apple orchards is believed to be in *The Odyssey* (900-800 BC). Meanwhile, Pliny, writing in the century before the birth of Christ, noted the practice of farmers auctioning apples while they still hung on their trees (this occurs in some Kent orchards to this day).

In what would one day become known as Britain, Neolithic men and women were familiar with the wild *Malus sylvestris*. Druids planted apple trees near their sacred oak groves, for spiritual rather than gastronomic reasons – historians believe that the trees served as hosts for the sacred mistletoe. It wasn't until the Romans settled in the British Isles that apple orchards were introduced – army veterans were rewarded for their service with land on which they grew fruits including apples.

When the Romans left and the Jutes, Saxons and Danes stepped into the breach, apple orchards

Traditional double handled cider mug

were abandoned along with the towns. However, those living in Christian monasteries kept the faith in more ways than one and managed to ensure their apple orchards continued to thrive. The Norman Conquest brought a telling change to apple cultivation. Backed with a strong tradition of apple growing and cider making, the Normans introduced many new types, including the Pearmain and the Costard – the latter eventually gave its name to the costermonger, originally a seller of Costard apples.

As war and plague raged, the Middle Ages saw a decline in fruit cultivation. This wasn't reversed until Henry VIII ascended the throne. His fruiter, one Richard Harris, started bringing in apple trees from France and oversaw the planting of a model orchard at Teynham in north Kent.

This growth of orchards continued throughout the 17th century, matched by an increasing market

Ornately engraved crystal cider glass from the 18th century

for cider. The end of the 18th century, however, saw a decline in fruit quality due to a mixture of canker and poor orchard management. In Herefordshire, it was more profitable to farm wheat and cattle. Attempts to protect the fruit market during the wars with France and high tariffs on imported fruit helped lead to an expansion of orchard planting in the 1820s and 1830s. However, when the tariffs were lowered in 1837, the seesaw nature of the apple market saw another collapse.

During the late 19th century fruit growing was approached more scientifically. Over in Herefordshire, the Woolhope Naturalists' Field Club began a survey of local orchards and between 1876 and 1885 the *Illustrated Herefordshire Pomona* was published. Members of the club saw the necessity in restoring Herefordshire to its true fruit-growing supremacy; they also wanted to call the attention of growers to the best varieties of fruit for the table and press as well as improving the methods of cider and perry manufacture. The Club distributed grafts of 92 different apple varieties and revived ancient but valued cider apples such as Foxwhelph and Skyme's Kernel. Varieties were also brought in from Normandy. Other technological innovations included the development of the fruit research centre at Long Ashton near Bristol in 1903. This eventually became known as the Long Ashton Research Station and continued its work until the 1980s.

Apple growing is now a much smaller industry than in the past, having declined steeply from its Victorian heyday; it has also been influenced by the growth of foreign imports. However, as long as craft cider is made in these Isles, our orchards will always shine with blossom come May and bear fruit in the autumn.

"I be 80 and never drinks nothin' but cider."

Cider making in the UK

Although apple orchards had been established since the days of the Roman legions, it was another group of invaders – the Normans – who introduced cider making to the British Isles. In the main apple growing counties including Kent, Somerset and Hampshire, most manors had their own cider presses and made their own cider, while monasteries regularly sold cider to the public. At Battle Abbey in Sussex, ironically at the site where Harold met his end, records from 1369 show three tuns of cider being sold for 55 shillings.

In medieval times, cider making was an important industry in Kent, and the area was noted for its strong and highly spiced version. Workers in monastery orchards in the 13th century received a daily allowance of cider as part of their wages, a practice that continued until very recently in the west of England.

In the 17th century, attention was paid to the apple varieties used for cider making and the quality of the cider. One author bemoaned the poor quality of the apples used in England while praising cider from Normandy and northern Spain. Things evidently hadn't improved by the end of the 18th century, when D Marshall, in his book *The Rural Economy of Gloucestershire*, lamented the poor quality of much of the cider produced in the county.

As he saw it, one of the faults was the way apples were harvested – men were sent out into the orchard with long thin poles to beat the fruit from the trees. 'Nature is the best judge,' he wrote, for deciding when an apple was ripe enough to fall from the tree. His book also gave much sensible advice on the storage of the fruit and its milling.

One of the methods of cider making condemned by Marshall was the production of *cuit cider*. This was described by A Fothergill, a physician commissioned to determine the extent of copper

Cider making equipment at Burrow Hill Cider, Somerset

contamination of ciders. He wrote: 'Cyder wine prepared after the method communicated by Dr Rush, as practised in America, viz by evaporating in a brewing copper the fresh apple-juice till half of it

Traditional harvesting of cider apples

have recourse to that odious article, bullock's blood, when the intention might be much better answered by whites of eggs, or isinglass.'

The writer concluded by highly recommending cider and perry produced by more straightforward traditional methods: 'When the must is prepared from the choicest fruit and undergoes the exact degree of vinous fermentation requisite to its perfection, the acid and the sweet are thus admirably blended with the aqueous, oily and spirituous principles, and the whole imbued with the grateful flavours of the rinds, and the agreeable aromatick butter of the kernels; it assumes a new character; grows lively, sparkling and exhilarating; and when completely mellowed by time, the liquor becomes at once highly delicious to the palate, and congenial to the constitution, superior in every respect to most other English wines, and perhaps not inferior to many of the foreign wines.'

be consumed. The remainder is then immediately conveyed into a wooden cooler, and afterwards is put into a proper cask, with an addition of yeast and fermented in the ordinary way. The process is evidently borrowed from what has long been practised on the recent juice of the grape, under the term of *vin cuit*, or boiled wine.'

The author condemned the process as a waste of both cider and fuel, and an obstacle to a full and complete fermentation, which then affected the quality of the cider. His report continued in the same vein,

Antique stone press

Following the attention given to the improvement of cider during the 18th century, there was much planting of cider apples in Herefordshire, Gloucestershire, Somerset and Devon. Cider was supplied to ships in Bristol harbour and

expressing disapproval at the inconsistency in production, especially the conduct of fermentation. Some cidermakers used open vats, others closed hogsheads, while some apparently tried to prevent fermentation under the impression that it was a fault. Then there was the fining of the liquor: 'Many

was often shipped by sea from Devon to London. Once in London it was sometimes adulterated and sold as imported wine.

Attention also began to be paid to cider apple varieties. The Foxwhelp became popular and was used in the finest ciders, while in Devon at the beginning of the 18th century the Royal Wilding became prominent. Somerset, not known for good cider until then, gave rise to the most famous cider apple of all, the Kingston Black (Black Taunton).

In the 19th century, much of the art of cider making which had developed during the previous two centuries seems to have been lost. It wasn't until 1898, when GW Radcliffe Cooke wrote *A Book about Cider and Perry*, that a revival of interest in cider apples began. At roughly the same time in Somerset, Neville Grenville, in co-operation with the Bath and West and Southern Counties Society, aided by small grants from the Board of Agriculture, began experiments on cider production. These experiments were one of the factors leading to the setting up of the National Fruit and Cider Institute.

In 1903, apple varieties included Foxwhelp in Herefordshire, Sweet Alford and Woodbine in Devon, and Morgan's Sweet and Kingston Black in Somerset. The National Fruit and Cider Institute

ran extensive trials in the mid 1930s leading to the widespread use of Yarlington Mill, a seedling raised in Somerset at the end of the 19th century.

The 20th century has led to a marked change in factory production of cider in Britain. Factories buy fruit from France and import apple juice from abroad, though the amount has declined in recent years. There has been some interest from the larger producers in locally-produced apples accompanied by a welcome improvement in the standard of cider.

However, the greatest change has been the resurrection and revival of small cider producers, all eager to follow the traditional modes of production – this revolution in cider making has mirrored the growth of the micro brewery in the world of beer. Thanks to a new set of pioneers and long-established family firms such as Westons, the choice of ciders available to drinkers has never been more varied.

With thanks to Gillian Grafton

Some cidermakers still use century-old oak vats for fermentation

Fermenting in modern stainless steel vats

Old tractor at Burrow Hill Farm, Somerset

The History of Perry

Pear growing in the UK

The ancestors of the pears that sit in our fruit bowls or are used to craft perry have, like the apple, also travelled a long way down the centuries. The first cultivated pear in Europe is thought to have been *Pyrus communis*, a native of Northern Asia. It is also found growing wild in Europe and Britain, but is generally doubted to be indigenous – could it have been brought here by the earliest travellers or merchants?

In the ancient worlds of Greek and Rome pears were commonplace: Cato the Elder, writing two centuries before Christ, named several varieties of pear. Pliny the Elder acted as an early consumer guide by insisting that Crustumian was the best variety and Falernian the most suitable for making wine. He also maintained it was harmful to eat pears raw and that they should be boiled with honey. This insistence that pears were injurious to health persisted in some parts of England in the 16th and 17th centuries.

Tacitus suggested that pears were cultivated when the Romans invaded the British Isles, but it isn't until the Domesday Book in 1086 that definite records are available. Old pear trees are mentioned several times as boundary markers, which implies cultivation for some time before this period. During the reign of Henry III (1207-72), records show that pears were imported from France, including the much-fêted ones from the La Rochelle area. Henry III's wife, Eleanor of Provence, also oversaw the extensive establishment of orchards, while in the reign of Henry's successor Edward I several pear varieties were noted. In 1388, Cistercian monks at Wardon in Bedfordshire introduced the first important English pear variety, the Wardon.

As well as furthering apple cultivation, Henry VIII's fruiterer Richard Harris introduced pears from across the Channel for planting at

Perry trees in a Gloucestershire orchard

Teynham. By the beginning of the 17th century new varieties were constantly being brought in from Europe and 129 were listed in 1691. The 17th century was also a time of other developments with Sir Thomas Hanmer and John Evelyn among the first to realise the value of grafting onto quince stock, which is now the preferred method of propagation.

The innovations continued. In 1770 one of the most important varieties still in cultivation today, Williams Bon Chrétien, was bred in Berkshire, while the start of the 19th century saw Thomas Andrew Knight developing pear varieties and the Royal Horticultural Society encouraging pear growing.

The need for correct growing conditions and a sufficient balance of rainfall and sunshine restrict the growing areas for perry pears in England to their traditional Three Counties heartland of Gloucestershire, Herefordshire and Worcestershire. This is where most of the indigenous varieties in use in perrymaking today have arisen.

The first English pears of note to arise from controlled breeding were Fertility (1875) and Improved Fertility (1934). Conference, the most widely planted commercial pear in England, was introduced in 1894. The breeding of pears at the research stations has not received the same attention as apples but some new varieties have been introduced. By the 1980s the number of varieties grown commercially became very limited and Conference is now the leading variety with smaller acreages of Doyenné du Comice and some Williams and Beurre Hardy. Craft perry makers have also planted a wide variety of perry pear trees as the market for perry has grown.

Perry making in the UK

It isn't until the Norman Conquest that we find evidence of perry making in the British Isles. This continued throughout the Middle Ages and by the late 16th century it was noted that *pirrie* (from the Saxon word *pirige* meaning a pear) was made from pears in Sussex, Kent, Worcestershire and other counties. The importance of the pear in Worcestershire was recognised by the incorporation of the three pears sable in Worcester city's arms.

Many of the pears grown in the 1600s, though astringent, were used for eating and cooking and the surplus sent to the mill. These include the Thorn Pear, the Hastings and Brown Bess. In the 19th century these were joined by the Cannock and Blakeney Red. Perry pears need sunshine and warmth and this dependence on good weather means that there are wide variations in vintage quality from year to year. This variation and the habit of some perry makers of using dessert pears (producing a thin, tasteless perry) led to the drink being held in low esteem.

Over the centuries the naming of pear varieties has led to confusion. Some varieties change name depending on where they are planted, even if in adjacent parishes and districts: for example the Rock variety is known as Mad Cap in the parish of Arlingham, Black Huffcap in Highnam, Brown Huffcap in Tibberton and Red Huffcap in Newent. Similarly, different parishes have given pears the same names despite being completely distinct varieties. An example of this is a pear generally known as the Red Pear – in most of the country you will be given the correct variety, but in Blakeney the pear called Red Pear is in fact the variety Blakeney Red, a quite different type. The confusion in naming reflects the restricted distribution of most varieties.

Despite this the names of perry pears are often vivid and colourful, in homage to to the perry they produce. Some of the most colourful examples are

Cider apples in the *Hertfordshire Pomona* of the 1860s

Merrylegs, Mumblehead, Lumberskull, Drunkers and Devildrink. The longest name on record is A Drop Of That Which Hangs Over The Wall.

The history of perry development in the UK is essentially the story of a few great men and of one highly influential but short-lived society. The first of these men was Thomas Andrew Knight. He has been called the father of modern scientific pomology and he carried out numerous physiological experiments on fruit trees. He also produced new varieties by selective breeding, and wrote the *Treatise on the Culture of the Apple and Pear* in 1797. He was one of the first to realise that perry quality depended on the vintage quality of the fruit. He published the landmark *Pomona Herefordiensis* in 1811, which describes the Holmer pear and four other vintage varieties.

Probably the greatest influence on perry development was the Woolhope Naturalists' Field Club, famous for its *Illustrated Herefordshire Pomona* (see p14). The Pomona describes 29 varieties of perry pear. There is also a chapter on renovation of orchards and the establishment of cider and perry factories by the Rev Charles Bulmer. His son, HP Bulmer, who founded the famous cider-making firm in 1887, took up this task.

Influenced by the Woolhope Club, R Neville Grenville and CW Radcliffe Cooke set up the National Fruit and Cider Institute in October 1903. The latter was elected as MP for Hereford and was known as the Member for Cider. He managed to prevent the government from imposing a tax on cider and perry, possibly even saving these industries as a result. His many articles were published in 1898 as *A Book about Cider and Perry*. He personally selected the perry pear Hellens Early which is still one of the best early varieties.

At the same time as the foundation of the National Fruit and Cider Institute, the actions of Herbert Edward Durham were having an influence. In the 1920s he surveyed the perry pears of Herefordshire and the lead labels he attached to the trees can still be seen across the West Midlands. He established a reference collection of 40 varieties at Bulmers' nurseries at Broxwood.

The last of the highly influential figures was BTP Barker. He was appointed director of the National Fruit and Cider Institute in 1904 and held the position for 38 years. Under his leadership the Institute developed into a state-funded world-renowned research institute. He established that the rootstock, climate, orchard management and soil conditions influenced the vintage quality of pears. An example of this is the Blakeney Red. Grown in the Severn flood plain, it was described by experts as fit only for the most ordinary purposes. However, grown on the high land of the Royal Forest of Dean, it yields excellent perry.

Perry pear 'Red Longdon'

In the late 1940s, Francis Showering, of the firm Showerings of Shepton Mallet, introduced modern perry-making processes. The company developed a market for perry (sold as Babycham) that created a demand for new orchard planting. It bought up farms around its factory in Somerset and began a planting programme.

After World War II, perry had an upmarket image – a bottle of sparkling perry became a must on many West Country dining tables and it was often served in a wine glass. Then along came Babycham, which turned perry into a frivolous party girl. Today perry is a minority drink and there are fewer than ten recognised perry varieties still grown, with Huffcap one of the favourites.

Fortunately, the resurrection of craft cider making has also helped to save perry from extinction. In its English heartlands of Herefordshire, Worcestershire and Gloucestershire, Minchew's, Gwatkin, Westons and Dunkertons produce small batches of perry. Somerset has an award-winning perry producer called Hecks. Meanwhile, over the border in Wales, Gwynt y Ddraig and Ralph's Cider also make award-winning perries.

Due to the the limited range of perry pears, perry will never reach the dizzying heights to which cider has climbed. However, at its best it has an elegance, versatility and complexity that the best beers and wines also possess – and that is why it will survive.

With thanks to Gillian Grafton

Pomona

Some apple and pear varieties

Brown's Apple
Sharp, harvested mid-October

Early sharp that originated from the village of Staverton in south Devon. It is harvested mid-October and has an acidic and astringent quality that makes it ideal to blend with bittersweets. The downside is that it can be bi-annual. Produces a fast fermenting juice. Kevin Minchew used it for the first time in cider-making 2008/2009. 'I've no idea what it will be like,' he says, 'but it should be interesting.' Brown's Apple is also used by Burrow Hill Cider and Butford Organics.

Burrow Hill Early
Bittersweet, harvested late September – early October

Early bittersweet rediscovered by Julian Temperley of Burrow Hill Cider (hence the name) back in the 1980s in an old orchard close to his farm in south Somerset. It is believed to be an older variety of apple, but no record of its original name has ever been found. Harvested end of September/early October, it produces a full-bodied and fruity cider, either on its own or as part of a blend.

Herefordshire Redstreak
Bittersharp, harvested early – mid-October

Bittersharp cider apple that made Herefordshire cider famous back in the 17th century, after being discovered growing wild in a field by Lord Scudamore. Supposed to have become extinct in the 1920s, though some nurseries are now offering young trees bearing its name for sale. According to acclaimed cider-maker Kevin Minchew, 'nobody knows what cider made with it tastes like'. One for the Indiana Joneses of cider.

Kingston Black
Bittersharp, harvested early November

Late mid-season bittersharp originally called Black Taunton; renamed after the village of Kingston St Mary near Taunton. Popular in the 19th century and listed in *Scott's Catalogue* (1873). Harvested early November. Bittersharp flavour with well-balanced tannin and acidity. Has found success as a full-bodied single-varietal cider from several producers, including Somerset-based Sheppy's and Hecks.

Tremlett's Bitter
Bittersweet, harvested October

Early bittersweet that originated in Devon but is now commonly grown in all cider producing counties, though some believe it doesn't do too well in Herefordshire. Has high tannin content and can either be used for a single-varietal (Sheppy's produce a regular one, as do Heck's while Thatchers do one from time to time) or in a blend. A big favourite of John Thatcher, though he does point out its one snag, that it's bi-annual.

Nehou
Bittersweet, harvested late September

Early bittersweet introduced into Herefordshire from France in the early part of the 20th century. Brought over by Bulmers, who, at the same time, sent over some of their apple varieties. Harvested late September. Has pleasant tannin levels and can produce a very dry cider. Chris Coles at Green Valley Cyder blends it with Morgan Sweet and has racked some into rum barrels for a seasonal cider Rum Tiddly Tum.

Red Longdon
Perry pear, harvested October

Perry pear that might have its origins in the village of Longdon in Worcestershire, though Kevin Minchew gets his supply from a tree near the Cotswolds town of Broadway. Is an old variety and harvested in October. Resembles Blakeney Red, though there are minute differences in perries made with the two. Kevin Minchew used it as part of a blend with Blakeney Red, Moorcroft and Brandy for his perry in 2007.

Somerset Redstreak
Bittersweet, harvested late September – mid-October

Early bittersweet with its origins in south-east Somerset. Harvested late September/mid October, though the apples have to be gathered in quickly after falling as deterioration can set in rapidly. Extensive planting has taken place since the 1970s. Produces pleasant and light single-varietal ciders that are popular starter ciders with novices. Try Perry's or Thatchers Somerset Redstreak single varietals. Some makers also prefer to blend them with several sharper varieties.

Strawberry Norman
Bittersweet, harvested October

Bittersweet apple grown in Herefordshire though the second part of the name means that it originally came from Normandy, probably in the 19th century. Also called Strawberry Hereford. Harvested in October. Can be found in the Thatchers collection, according to John Thatcher, but is no longer commercially grown. Where available is used in blending, and has been used by producers such as Dunkertons, Malvern Magic and Seidr O Sir. Gwynt y Ddraig experimented with making a single varietal draft cider in 2007, but are currently unable to produce a bottled version due to the difficulty of sourcing enough apples.

Tom Putt
Dual-purpose, harvested early September

Early dual-purpose apple that can also taste well when cooked. Doubts remain over where it was first grown, with Somerset, Dorset and Devon all laying claim to crops in the 18th century. Harvested early September. Ideal for a clean-tasting cider with a brisk sharpness.

Major
Bittersweet, harvested late September – early October

Found in both central Somerset and in Devon, south of the Blackdown Hills. It is an early bittersweet and there are records of it being planted in trial orchards in the years before the First World War. It is harvested late September/early October, which makes it a good apple for early cider. Chris Cole at the award-winning Green Valley Cyder blends it with Ashton Bitter for a 'nice well-balanced cider'.

Yarlington Mill
Bittersweet, harvested late October – early November

Late mid-season bittersweet that was first noted in the late 19th century in the eastern Somerset village of Yarlington; reputedly discovered growing out of the wall near a waterwheel. Harvested late October/ early November. It is grown in many parts of Somerset and produces a sweetish, slightly astringent cider if used on its own (ironically enough, usually by Herefordshire cider-makers), though it is also found in blends. Gwynt y Ddraig make a single varietal, and Gwatkin's single varietal Yarlington Mill took home gold at CAMRA's National Cider and Perry Championships in 2002.

Pile of cider apples ready for the press at Sheppy's Cider, Somerset

Cidermaking

How Cider is Made

Nothing could be easier than making cider. You simply mill apples (or pears to make that rarest of treats, perry) to a pulp and squeeze the resulting mass in a press to extract the juice. Seal the juice into big barrels to ferment slowly over the winter, and you have cider.

And at its most basic, making cider really is that simple. (Or cyder – the spellings are actually interchangeable, whatever the mythmakers may tell you. The difference is in fact purely orthographic: in the 18th century the long 'y' perfectly acceptable to Shakespeare became pretty much obsolete and was generally replaced by a long 'i'. Blake's 'Tyger, Tyger' is the last literary use of the long 'y' I can think of – but obviously cidermakers were no orthographers!) You can use any old apples – dessert apples, cooking apples, even crab apples – provided they're not rotten; you don't even need to add yeast – nature will provide that for you. (Perry is more tricky: culinary pears don't generally make good perry and you really do need to use specially-cultured varieties.) Let the cider ferment slowly at a low temperature over the winter, and by early summer you should have a plentiful supply of a dry, still, refreshing golden apple wine that's as pure and natural as can be.

You probably won't, though. You'll probably end up with a sour, murky liquid that needs hefty dosing with lemonade to make it even remotely potable. Because to make consistently excellent cider you need special apples, special equipment and special expertise.

Cider, naturally, starts with the apple – and the varieties most commonly used to make cider are nothing like the ones you eat or cook with. In East Anglia, Kent and Sussex, cidermakers do use dessert and cooking apples but, in the West Country and Hereford and Worcester, where most British cider is produced, they use special strains high in malic acid and tannin. To bite into one is a mouth-puckering experience.

Cider apple 'Knotted Kernel'

These varieties, with characterful names such as Slack-ma-girdle, Foxwhelp, Yarlington Mill, Brown Snout and Tom Putt, are in the main the direct descendants of the Pearmain and Costard apples introduced soon after the Norman Conquest, although the gene pool has since been periodically refreshed with the importation of other types.

Cider apple varieties – and there are more than 300 of them, although only a couple of dozen are cultivated on a commercial scale – fall into four categories, according to the balance of tannin and acid they contain. Bittersweets are high in tannin and lower in acid; sharps are low in tannin and higher in acid; bittersharps are high in both; and sweets are low in both. Most traditional ciders contain proportions of all four, and much of the skill of the cidermaker lies in the blending. Some makers choose their blend before processing, and mill all the different varieties together. Others press each

> **The varieties of apple most commonly used to make cider are nothing like the ones you eat or cook with**

variety separately and judiciously blend the different juices before fermenting, or they ferment the different varieties separately and then blend. Some makers have even given up blending and sell at least some of their ciders as single varietals. This is by and large a modern trend which is dismissed as a marketing gimmick by many traditionalists: few varieties, they say, are sufficiently complex and balanced to make a decent cider on their own. However, it's worth noting that some varieties, especially the Somerset Redstreak, were thought rounded enough to produce single varietal ciders as long ago as the 18th century.

Whether sharp or sweet, cider apples have one thing in common: they're tough little beggars, and they don't give up their juice easily. Singly, you can crush one by stamping on it. En masse, they have frightening compressive strength. The press has not been built that will extract the juice from a heap of uncrushed apples – first they have to be minced, milled or sliced into a pulp.

The earliest device for crushing the apples to form a sticky mass of 'pomace' seems to have been an oversized pestle and mortar. In the cider museum at Valognes in Normandy you can see one made of stone, about the size of a baby bath but deeper, in which the apples were pounded with a big wooden *pilon* shaped like a baseball bat. This could date from any time in history: mechanical versions, including one in which the pestle was replaced by a stone rocker, come from the 17th century. But within living memory some very small-scale English makers used a cut-down barrel and a piece of 4x4 for the same purpose; the apples were crushed inside a sack to stop the pomace from spraying all over the place.

This simple apparatus was undoubtedly effective but must have been equally laborious. In the 17th century it was superseded by the horse-operated mill which could crush far more apples far more quickly and with far less labour. In many barns and farmyards in Britain's western cider-producing regions (and, for that matter, in Normandy), you can still find a circular trough of rough-cut stone. Imagine that at the centre of the ring formed by the trough there's a big upright beam with a long horizontal axle attached. At the far end of the axle, outside the circumference of the trough, there's a horse or a donkey. Standing upright in the middle of the axle, with its rim sitting snugly inside the trough, is a millstone. Fill the trough with apples, gee up your horse, and in next to no time you'll have a goodly stock of pomace all ready for the press.

Modern cider making equipment at Sheppy's Cider, Tauton

Very boring, not to say dizzying, for the horse, but a supremely simple and efficient piece of machinery, and useful not only for crushing apples, either: renowned traveller Celia Fiennes reported seeing a horse mill being used to crush woad for dye at Toddington, Gloucestershire, in 1694.

The more modern alternative to the crushing mill is the 'scratter' or 'scratcher' – a row of rotating circular blades on an axle mounted inside a hopper. Scratters come in all shapes and sizes, and even some small commercial operators still use hand-cranked ones, which take some effort to operate but can mince up a surprising volume of apples in a day's hard physical labour. Mechanical scratters come in all sizes – from the domestic to industrial versions that can process 12 tons of apple an hour and more. (I have also seen apples crushed in a giant version of a standard household mincing machine – basically a hopper with a pipe fixed to its bottom fitted with a worm or augur. This however, was in a vineyard that makes cider as a sideline, and was improvised from standard wine-making equipment.)

After the crushing, the pressing. I confess I have no idea how this was managed in ancient times. Screw presses were, however, known to Pliny the Elder (23–79 AD) and are thought to have been invented by the Romans in the first century BC. They were used all over the Empire to press both grapes and olives, but after that knowledge of them seems to have died out in Northern Europe until the 12th century. Scew presses proved very suitable for pressing pomace, and remained basically unchanged until modern times. The basic design is a flatbed with a framework above it on which a heavy press, turned by a screw, is mounted. The pomace is built up in layers on the flatbed, and has to be wrapped to prevent the juice from squirting out sideways as the screw is turned. Some makers pile the pomace between fine mesh 'hairs', originally of actual horsehair but now of hessian or polyester, while others form it into 'cheeses' of alternate layers of pomace and straw. Both methods have their apologists.

Bigger and more modern makers have replaced their old screw presses with belt-presses on which a continuous stream of pomace is fed onto a conveyor belt that passes between stainless steel rollers. Traditionalists claim this affects the flavour of the cider, but it's the only viable way the major manufacturers can process the quantities of pomace they have to handle. It's much faster, more efficient and more cost-effective than the old way – but it's not as picturesque.

The next and final step is to turn it into cider through the mystery of fermentation. Well, it's not a mystery any more, not since Louis Pasteur discovered yeast. But before then, nobody really knew what happened once the juice was sealed into barrels for the winter. Yeast, a fungus-like micro-organism, gets to work on the sugars present in the juice, breaking them down into carbon dioxide and alcohol. Yeast is naturally present in the apples – in fact, it's naturally present almost everywhere – and some makers just leave the natural yeast to get on with it. Others prefer to kill off the natural with chemicals and substitute a dose of cultured yeast for a more predictable result.

The first fermentation is quite dramatic, producing a thick, orange-tinged, rocky head and a clearly audible hiss of CO_2. But it soon exhausts its first burst of energy, and at this point the cider is usually (although not necessarily) drawn off into a clean vessel for its long, slow, secondary fermentation. The vessels in which the secondary fermentation takes place are usually kept in unheated barns or even outdoors: the low winter temperature slows the process down and makes for a smoother finished product. Secondary fermentation or conditioning can last for five or six months, during

Pressing apples at Oliver's Cider, Herefordshire

which time much of the apple's sharp malic acid is transformed into richer, mellower lactic acid.

By the time the cider is ready to drink almost all the sugar should have been digested, giving a cider of 7 or 8% alcohol by volume or sometimes even more, depending on the amount of sunshine during the apples' growing season. A fully-fermented cider will be almost completely dry and will be still rather than fizzy, its natural CO_2 having entirely dissipated.

And that's pretty much that. Of course, there are variations: you can make a naturally sweet cider, as the Normans do, by adding a dose of lime to precipitate the proteins the yeast needs, and racking the cider from barrel to barrel to discourage the surviving yeast from reproducing. You can make it naturally fizzy simply by bottling it before fermentation has finished, or by the more cumbersome *méthode champenoise* – dosing each bottle with a little yeast and sugar, letting it start working again, then freezing the neck of the bottle and removing the lees in a single lump. But basically what you have when you make cider the traditional way is a pure, natural product as subtle and refined as any wine.

Unfortunately, very little of the cider you are likely to encounter – five per cent of the country's entire output, if that – will match the above description. The old way of making cider might be the simplest, but it is utterly unsuited to the demands of an industrial machine the size of Bulmers or Gaymer's. It's too expensive, too slow, and altogether too risky. These makers need to bring to market a consistent product that's identical from batch to batch and year to year – but traditionally-made cider is a vintage product that varies dramatically in strength and character from crop to crop.

So, commercial producers use a great deal of reconstituted apple concentrate rather than freshly-pressed pure juice, both to keep costs down and to maintain production throughout the year. They chaptalise it – artificially boost the sugar levels of the juice before fermentation – and then water down the resulting liquid to get the same strength batch after batch. They then pasteurise their cider for a long shelf life, often creating a nasty caramel off-flavour in the process. (And this is despite the fact that natural cider is remarkably long-lived, even after the barrel has been broached. In the days of sail many captains took barrels of cider to sea knowing that even at the end of a long voyage the last drop would be almost as good as the first. It also helped counteract scurvy). Commercial cider is also filtered to remove the natural pectin haze, which can range from a faint opalescence to an impenetrable opacity and accounts for the cloudiness of much farm cider.

Finally, the cider is artificially carbonated, turning what should be a completely still drink into a fizzy one. Cider can be made naturally sparkling by either of the methods described above (and until 1975, Bulmers put the fizz into its Pomagne brand by the *méthode champenoise*). However, the vast majority of commercial cider is artificially carbonated, even the better brands such as Thatchers and Sheppy's single-varietal bottled ranges. The only nationally-distributed still ciders I know of are some Weston's

brands and the Co-op's excellent Tillington Hills Dry Reserve, made from apples grown in its Herefordshire orchard. But cider has been habitually carbonated for so long now – since before the war, in fact – that most people don't even realise that in its natural state it has nary a bubble.

Perhaps this book will help you discover cider as it ought to be.

Above and below: Wilkins Cider, Somerset. Apples waiting to be loaded onto the elevator and preparing the 'cheeses' ready for the press.

Collecting apples at Newton Court Cider, Herefordshire

The Cidermakers'
Calendar – Autumn

The cidermaker's year, like the school year, starts in September when the apple harvest gets under way in earnest and the business of making cider can begin.

Picking apples in any quantity isn't easy, especially in old-style orchards where climbing to the tops of the trees with a basket is hardly an economic option. And waiting for the wind to do its work would be a long and unpredictable business, although windfalls can be and are collected for cidermaking.

Traditionally, workers with long hooked poles simply shook the branches, while others collected the fruit as it fell. The apples would either be gathered into heaps or 'tumps' to mature and soften for a few days or taken straight to the mill. Here they would be floated in troughs or even streams to wash away any leaves, twigs and sundry insects, and to allow the apples to be inspected so that rotten fruit could be discarded (you can make perfectly passable cider out of fruit that is merely bruised, but not if it has started to rot).

More modern bush orchards, which can support 250 trees to the acre compared to the standard orchard's 40, are harvested mechanically. They're planted in rows wide enough to allow the passage of a machine that clamps the trunks and then vibrates rather than shakes them – shaking loosens the roots and damages the trees. The first machine is followed by a blower that drives the fallen fruit from under the trees into the central lane, where it's picked up by a third machine with rotating rubber paddles which flip the apples into collecting bags.

Cidermaking starts later these days than it used to: in olden days early-cropping sweet varieties were picked and pressed in summer to make a light cider that would be ready for Christmas. Indeed one of the many reasons why there are so many cider apple varieties is to allow growers to plant varieties that crop at different times, stretching the harvest from late summer right through to early December and spreading the work over four or five months. Nowadays, though, the harvesting, milling and pressing takes place from mid-September to mid-November.

Heron Valley Organic Juices – feeding the cows with the used pomace in autumn

The Cidermakers'
Calendar – Winter

Winter is a time of patience for the cidermaker. The apples are all milled and pressed, and put to rest in their fermenters. There's nothing to do in the factory but leave the yeast to its business. Out in the orchards, though, there's plenty of work. Once the leaves have fallen it's time for pruning – a vital task in preparation for next year's crop. All the apples, not just those at the top of the tree, need sunlight. They need air, too, to dry them after rain, and space to minimise the spread of mildews and moulds.

Pruning is a big job, for a tidy tree is a healthy and productive tree. The increasingly common sight of unpruned and unkempt orchards is a melancholy one for the cider lover. In fact, the acreage of commercial orchards in Britain fell from 150,000 in 1970 to only 50,000 by the turn of the century. It's on the increase again now, thanks to the planting of thousands of acres of cider orchards mainly by the bigger manufacturers, so there's still plenty of pruning to do in January and February.

Rob Uren of Malvern Magic Cider, Herefordshire
pruning apple trees in February

The *Cidermakers'* Calendar – *Spring*

By spring, the new cider should be ready for drinking. Some ciders are matured for much longer than a single winter – indeed the last of the previous season's cider, now a year old, will probably still be in stock, and will still be perfectly good. But late spring is the time when the new season's cider goes on sale – another reason for calling May the merrie, merrie month.

This is also blossom time – that spectacular season when the countryside froths with pink and white flowers. Beekeepers with their hives are important springtime visitors to the orchards – the blossom provides a welcome early feast for the bees, which in return do the essential work of pollination. And it's not just bees that are attracted to the blossoming orchards: coach operators used to run blossom-time tours of apple-growing regions, although the loss of orchards in the last 40 years would make for a much less spectacular excursion than in previous times.

But one tour that every cider lover should make is of Herefordshire in early April, when the perry pear trees are in blossom. Perry pear trees blossom earlier than apple trees, and the sight of these majestic trees the size of oaks or elms, snowy with flowers when all around is still bare and winterbound, is a glorious herald of returning life. Traditionally, these trees were grown not in orchards but singly, in the cow pastures, since one or two of the giant trees would provide all the fruit a farmer needed.

However, for the grower, blossom time is a time of anxiety. A late frost could ruin the harvest by killing the blossom (the origin of the expression 'nipped in the bud'), and a wet spring can stop the fruit from setting.

Apple blossom in spring at the Upton Cider Company, Oxfordshire

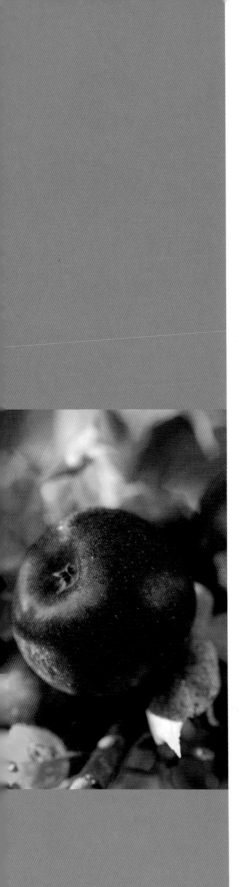

The *Cidermakers'* Calendar – *Summer*

Given a temperate spring, the cidermaker can afford to relax a little in the summer months and watch the apples swell and ripen. It wasn't always thus – country lore gives St Swithun's Day, 15th July, as the date when early sweets might be ready to pick. Nowadays, though, many cidermakers buy in dessert apples such as Cox's to provide the sugars their juice needs, rather than grow their own sweet cider varieties.

Even so, summer can't be entirely given over to relaxation. For apples aren't the only organisms to burgeon in the sunshine: pests thrive in the summer as much as the fruit does, and now is the time for spraying. Many modern growers have gone back to the old way of complementary planting, circling their orchards with hedgerows that provide habitat for predators, who will keep the pest population down. Still, some degree of spraying is still generally considered indispensable, even in organic orchards, where insecticides based on natural plant extracts such as pyrethrum and nicotine are permitted.

For owners of standard orchards (those with old-fashioned tall trees rather than modern bush trees), there's also some money to be made in summer when the grazing can be let out to stockbreeders. Sheep, cattle and pigs all thrive on orchard grass and windfalls; they also oblige the grower by manuring the ground and by keeping down prolific weeds, especially brambles, that otherwise hinder the harvest.

Apple orchards in summer at Brimblecombe's Cider Farm, Devon

Apple Day

As well as the natural cycle of the seasons and the tasks and rewards they bring, there are two key dates in the cidermaker's calendar: Apple Day in late October and Wassailing in mid January.

It can't be easy creating a new event in the nation's festive calendar, especially for a tiny charity with almost no resources. But in a country that doesn't even recognise its own saint's day as a national holiday, Common Ground has done exactly that.

Common Ground's unique mission is to create a link between the arts and the environment, and in its 30-odd years it has proved remarkably successful. Among its whirlwind of activities it publishes books; it works with natural artists such as Andy Goldsworthy and the photographer James Ravilious, now sadly departed; it helps create and protect community orchards; and it is part of the Campaign for Local Distinctiveness.

And on Sunday 21st October 1990, in Covent Garden, it held the nation's first Apple Day. The event was publicised in advance by a marquee in the Piazza containing an exhibition of Ravilious's West Country orchard photographs and a table with 100 apple varieties on it. The attention attracted by the marquee ensured that come

the day itself the Piazza was crowded with literally thousands of people, and the attractions laid on by Common Ground formed a prototype for today's Apple Day events all over Britain. Centrepiece was a cidermaker hard at work with an enormous wooden press; there was apple identification, a cider bar, nurserymen with rare apple varieties and trees for sale, even a display laid on by a North London school that had its own orchard and beehives.

'We wanted to reach out as widely as possible and give this event to people and communities,' says Common Ground's Sue Clifford. 'We didn't want to hold it again ourselves, although we weren't short of requests. We wanted it to become a national custom and we wanted people to plan and hold Apple Day celebrations of their own.'

In October 1991 about 50 Apple Day events were staged, with attractions inspired by the original. By 2000 the number had risen to 600, and Common Ground stopped counting.

'We put about 400 of the biggest events on our website, but we know there are many more than that,' says Sue. 'We help with ideas and publicity, but Apple Day belongs to the people. There are many events we're never even told about. We wanted to create a calendar custom, and I've even heard it being called Traditional Apple Day, so I suppose we've succeeded!'

Wassailing

Charging round outdoors in the middle of the night yelling at the top of your voice, banging pots and pans, and even firing off shotguns might sound like a suitable case for an ASBO. And if it happened anywhere other than a cider orchard in January, it obviously would be. But there's a time and a place for everything, and what we're talking about here isn't an extreme example of rustic antisocial behaviour, but the (possibly) ancient and (certainly) very necessary ceremony of wassailing.

'Wassail' is a truly great word that conjures up images of historic carousals. Anglo-Saxons downing mead by the gallon, lusty medieval carol singers, Elizabethan servitors carving slices off roast pigs' heads, great steaming bowls of spiced ale with baked crab apples floating in them – it's all there. The word simply means 'good health' (literally, 'be hale') and is said to be Anglo-Saxon or Anglo-Danish in origin.

In the later Middle Ages, the word meant both a carol and a feast celebrating the New Year, as well as the drink of hot spiced ale and roast crab apples also known as lambs wool. Only in the late 16th century was the word wassailing used specifically to refer to late-night shenanigans in wintry orchards.

So what is wassailing (or, in some regions, howling, yowling, or souling)?

Essentially, a group of cidermakers and their friends and relations gather either on Twelfth Night (6th January) or more commonly Old Twelfth Night (17th January) for a big party. At or about midnight, they rush out into the orchard singing one of the many regional variants of The Wassailing Song, and banging pots and pans to frighten off any lurking devils. An offering of toast is placed in the fork of the biggest tree in the orchard; cider is poured on to its roots; and finally a shotgun volley is fired into its upper branches – safely over the head, one hopes, of the small boy who in some versions of the ceremony is hoisted into the lower branches to be fed with bread, cheese and (of course) cider.

Where it all comes from, nobody knows. Clearly it's a demon-scaring, crop-blessing, good-luck ceremony that romantics like to think of as a survival from our pagan past, driven underground by Christian persecutors but always bubbling to the surface again. The trouble with this and other persecuted underground paganism theories, though, is that the pagans understandably committed nothing to paper, so we can't say anything about them for sure, not even that they ever existed.

More hard-headed historians consider wassailing to have started as an outdoors overspill of the exuberant parties that marked the end of the Twelve Days – and it's notable that that first mention, from Kent in 1585, describes its celebrants as groups of young men. The defining features of the modern wassail – carol-singing, kettle-bashing, and firearms – were gradually added over the years, but the basis was a cocktail of booze, testosterone and youth.

So maybe, then, wassailing is more about high spirits than evil spirits. But hey – have you ever come across a demon in a cider orchard? Of course not. Obviously, then, wassailing works.

Apple orchards provide us with cider, but they also provide us with mistletoe. The evergreen leaves and branches with their pearly-white berries are a traditional symbol at Christmas, and the mistletoe harvest – essential for apple growers needing to protect their trees from this parasite – also provides an extra cash crop in winter. Druids first planted apple trees as hosts for their sacred mistletoe, and a tour round the cider orchards of the Three Counties and the Southwest will reveal that, whilst apple trees may nowadays be appreciated for their apples, their festive guest is very much still in evidence.

Cider Events through the Year

Cider and perrymakers have a year-round commitment to their occupation – and so too do cider enthusiasts. As the annual traditions of blossomtime, harvest, wassail and the broaching of the first cider cask come round, cider drinkers can get hands-on with their favourite natural and seasonal drink – visiting the farms where it's made and meeting the producers at shows and events through the year.

Please be aware that whilst every effort has been made to check the accuracy of this listing, it is by no means comprehensive, and there is no guarantee that these festivals will be occurring on an annual basis.

Spring

Blossomtime
Every spring, cider enthusiasts flock to Putley in Herefordshire, where the Big Apple Association holds its Blossomtime festival, incorporating the annual Cider and Perry trials and a chance to meet cider-makers.

Early May bank holiday weekend, see www.bigapple.org.uk for details.

CAMRA National Cider and Perry Championships
Hosted by the Reading Beer and Cider Festival, cider and perry judging starts on Friday, with the winner announced on Saturday afternoon. The festival typically features over 150 ciders and perries as well as over 450 cask beers.

Early May bank holiday weekend, see www.readingbeerfestival.org.uk for details.

Devon County Show
The county's biggest annual event, the show features food and drink producers, alongside livestock and agricultural awards. The beer tent features ciders from many of Devon's producers.

Late May, see www.devoncountyshow.co.uk for details.

The Royal Bath & West Show
The country's most popular agricultural event holds a cider and perry trials, as well as stocking numerous ciders and perries to buy.

Late May, see www.bathandwest.com for details.

The Welsh Perry & Cider Festival
The society's premier event, held at the Clytha Inn in Abergavenny, where visitors can try ciders and perries from all of the society's members in the beautiful south Wales countryside.

Late May bank holiday weekend, see www.welshcider.co.uk for details.

Summer

Three Counties Show
Held at the Malvern Showground in Worcester, home of the National Collection of Perry Pears, the Three Counties Cider & Perry Association run a bar featuring numerous local ciders and perries to try and buy.

Mid June, see www.threecounties.co.uk/threecounties for details.

Ross-on-Wye cider festival
Cider pressing, music and a ceilidh at Broome Farm in Ross-on-Wye, Herefordshire, as well as an opportunity to meet guest cidermakers and try their ciders and perries on the Saturday, and a farmers market on the Sunday.

Late August/early September, see www.rosscider.com for details.

Autumn

Cider month

October has been designated Cider month by CAMRA, and various cider-related events are held around the country, as well as the announcement of the National Cider Pub of the Year.

October, see www.camra.org.uk/cidermonth for details.

The Big Apple

Every autumn, the tiny parishes on the Marcle Ridge in Herefordshire put on a celebration of harvestime and of their apple growing and cider-making traditions, centering on the village of Much Marcle.

Early October, see www.bigapple.org.uk/autumntime for details.

Apple day

21st October is Apple Day, and hundreds of events are held around the country on or near this date to mark our newest traditional holiday. Started by Common Ground in 1990, Apple Day has been embraced by cidermakers nationwide.

Mid-October, see www.commonground.org.uk/appleday for details.

Cidermaking festival

The Cider Museum in Hereford hosts demonstrations of traditional cider making, blacksmithing, woodland crafts and textile weaving. Display of apples, and tutored cider tastings, with free samples of cider.

Mid-October, see www.cidermuseum.co.uk for details.

La Faîs'sie d'Cidre

This annual two-day event in Hamptonne celebrates Jersey's heritage of apple cultivation and cider making, including the spectacle of tonnes of apples being crushed in the traditional way as well as cider tastings and talks about cider.

Mid-October, see www.jerseyheritagetrust.org for details.

Ralph's cidermaking festival

A working weekend at Ralph's cider farm in New Radnor, Powys, where Ralph's collection of Victorian scratters, apple mills and screw presses will be pressed into use to press this year's apple harvest.

Mid-October, see www.ralphsciderfestival.co.uk for details.

Cidermaking day

Mill House Cider Museum holds two days of traditional cider making demonstrations over October half-term, using both antique and simple home-made equipment

Late October, see www.millhousecider.co.uk for details.

Winter

Wassail

The traditional cider-drinkers and producer's welcoming in of the new year. Wassail events are held by cidermakers and orcharders up and down the country on 12th night.

Early January, see www.england-in-particular.info for a list of events near you.

Britain's Cider Regions

Cider can be made wherever apples grow. And historically, it was. There are 13th-century records of cider being made not only in its modern heartland: the West Midlands and South-Western England, but in Norfolk, Kent, Surrey, Sussex, Bedfordshire, Buckinghamshire, even Yorkshire. And today there are small independent commercial makers in Glamorgan, Monmouthshire, Radnorshire, Berkshire, Oxfordshire, Cheshire, Shropshire, Cambridgeshire, Northamptonshire, Dorset, Wiltshire and the Isle of Wight. There have even been attempts at making cider in fruit-growing Tayside, which have been frustrated more by lack of customers than by any practical consideration.

But the two main cider producing regions remain as they always were. Geographers define England and Wales as two topographic halves, divided by the Axe-Tees line. East of it there are principal cider-producing regions in East Anglia and Kent, Sussex and Surrey; west of it there are the 'three counties' – Herefordshire, Worcestershire and Gloucestershire; and the South-West – Somerset, Devon and Cornwall.

East and west have very different traditions. Rainfall is lower on the eastern side of the Axe-Tees line, and the soil is lighter. For centuries the eastern counties have grown culinary and dessert apples for the London market, using their misshapes and seconds to make light, dry and, thanks to the high sugar content of dessert apples, notably alcoholic ciders (they tend to range from 6.5 to 8.5% alcohol by volume compared to the 6 to 7.5% abv more common in the west). But in the east, cider production on a commercial scale was held back by dense populations, good communications and plentiful arable, which all made beer brewing the more viable alternative.

To the west of the Axe-Tees line, heavier soils and greater rainfall proved more suitable for cider varieties, economically grown in orchards that doubled as summer pasture for cattle and sheep. The preponderance of hill country in the western counties proved good for cidermakers, too – sloping ground makes better orchards than cornfields, and the comparative shortage of flat arable land put a limit on barley

Newcastle Upon Tyne

Carlisle

Durham

Sunderland

Isle of Man

Middlesbrough

Valley Bar, Scarborough

York Beer & Wine Shop

Irish Sea

Blackpool

Preston

Bradford

Leeds

Kingston upon Hull

Manchester

Liverpool

Doncaster

Scunthorpe

The Cider Centre

Sheffield

Anglesey

Bangor

Chester

Lincoln

Old Poets' Corner

Steve Hughes

Wrexham

Stoke-on-Trent

Nottingham

Whin Hill Cider

King's Lynn

Norwich

Great Yarmouth

MONTGOMERY- SHIRE

Shrewsbury

Leicester

Peterborough

NORFOLK

Cardigan Bay

The Cider House

Birmingham

Crone's Organic Cider

RADNOR- SHIRE

Kidderminster

WORCESTSHIRE

CAMBRIDGESHIRE

Northampton

Cambridge

SUFFOLK

Ralph's Cider & Perry

Butford Organics

Teme Valley Market

Worcester

Bedford

Ipswich

Hereford Cider Museum, Hereford

The Cider House

BRACKNOCK- SHIRE

Ross-on-Wye Cider & Perry

Minchew's Real Cyder & Perry

Stevenage

Colchester

Cheltenham

Gloucester

Oxford

St. Albans

Chelmsford

Miners Arms

GLOUCESTSHIRE

Stroud Farmers' Market

Thames

LONDON

Brogdale Horticultural Trust

Swansea

Newport

Swindon

Borough Market

Greenwich Covered Market

Canterbury

Gwynt y Ddraig

Cardiff

Bristol's Slow Food Market

Reading

SURREY

Maidstone

KENT

Bristol Channel

Bath

Wilkins Cider

Andover

Guilford

Royal Tunbridge Wells

Dover

Folkestone

SOMERSET

Somerset Rural Life Museum

Crawley

Sedlescombe Organic Vinyard

Bristol & Exeter Inn, Bridgewater

Hecks Farmhouse Cider

Southampton

SUSSEX

National Collection of Cider & Perry

Taunton

Burrow Hill Cider

Yeovil

Brighton

Chichester

Eastbourne

DEVON

Bournemouth

Portsmouth

Brimblecombe's Cider

Exeter

Green Valley Complex

Dorchester

Isle of Wight

Square & Compass

Ye Olde Cider Bar

Torquay

English Channel

Plymouth

N

Channel Islands

0   25   50 miles

pubs and cider houses

places

producers

outlets

cider regions

production. More scattered rural populations and poorer communications also gave cidermaking the competitive edge over beer brewing.

And thus it remains today. Taken together, the Three Counties and the South-West are easily Europe's largest cider-making region, containing both of the country's surviving volume manufacturers and half-a-dozen or so big independents but only one old-established independent brewery. By contrast, the eastern cidermaking counties have only three independent cidermakers of any size, compared to seven old-established independent breweries.

The Three Counties

Herefordshire, Worcestershire and Gloucestershire have a strong claim to being the heartland of the modern English cider industry – with Hereford its capital city. Whether the region makes more cider than the South-West, and whether cidermaking has a longer history here than in East Anglia, nobody knows for sure. But there's no doubt that the industrialisation of what had been a purely agrarian pursuit and the development of cider as most people know it happened here first.

Leaving aside the rugged uplands of the extreme west of Herefordshire and the high plateaux and

Picking windfall apples at harvest time, Ross on Wye Cider and Perry, Herefordshire

The Cider Route

Proper cider and perry, made with apples and pears and nothing but, is a wonderful drink. But there's so much more to it than that. It has lore and legend, magic and mystique. More than any other native British beverage, it connects the drinker with the countryside, with the country people of the past and the customs and beliefs of a world just beyond our own.

Newton Court Cider, Herefordshire

To experience all this for yourself you must do more than merely drink. You must visit the ancient orchards and speak to the people who tend them, who live in and on them. And there is no better way of doing this than visiting Herefordshire and taking advantage of the route that the county's tourist board has thoughtfully laid out.

It's a long route, starting in Hereford itself, the very navel of the shire, and embracing, in a tortuous circuit of the county boundary, 15 cidermakers from the smallest to the largest (or almost the largest – the one place you won't be calling at is Bulmer's), from the oldest to the newest.

The tour begins at the cider museum and King Offa distillery in the sandstone city. Then it snakes west-north-west up the Wye valley, calling first at the aptly-named Orgasmic Cider Company before reaching picturesque Pembridge and Dunkerton's. Brooke Farm, Newton Court, Butford Farm – the roll-call of cideries goes on as the tour takes you to Leominster, Ledbury, the edge of the majestic Malverns, Much Marcle, Ross-on-Wye and the Golden Valley with its ruined abbey of gold, Abbeydore, before returning to Hereford and its red cathedral.

You could drive it in a morning, for Herefordshire is physically not a large county. Or you could eke it out in leisurely stages, to last a lifetime of romance and imagination, for Herefordshire has enough of these and more.

Or you could forsake your car and take to two wheels, for two cycling routes of about 20 miles each have also been planned for you. One starts and ends in Ledbury, visiting Ledbury Cider & Perry, Weston's, Gregg's Pit, and Lyne Down. You could base yourself in the historic Feathers in Ledbury, one the country's finest half-timbered coaching inns, or at the cosier Talbot, and visit the Prince of Wales, one of the most photographed pubs in Britain.

The second route revolves around Pembridge, where the ancient New Inn boasts a huge settle carved out of the town's old cockpit, and where the tiny covered yarn-market still stands in the tiny market square. Dunkerton's is the only cider mill on the route; but if you care for some farm-made cheese to accompany your cider it also takes in Monkland Dairy.

Details of the tour and the two cycle routes are to be found at www.ciderroute.co.uk

Kevin Minchew harvesting perry pears from his trees

Cidermaking here was, as elsewhere, originally a secondary use of pastureland conducted only on a domestic scale. But after the medieval period the richness of the soil attracted waves of improvers, starting with Viscount Scudamore in the 17th century and going through to Radcliffe Cooke in the 19th century, whose attentions meant continual development both of the strains of cider fruit and the methods of husbandry, and also in the technology of cidermaking itself. The quality and quantity of the output, coupled with the expansion of the canal network, made Herefordshire cider a popular drink as far away as London in the 18th century. London investors even considered it worth buying up Herefordshire orchards.

The real industrialisation of cider, though, can be pinpointed to a precise moment in history and an equally precise geographical location: in late 1888 Percy Bulmer, the son of the Vicar of Credenhill and with no roots in farming, moved his fledgling cider firm from Maylord Street in Hereford to Ryelands Street, which was to be its home for more than a century. Within a few years the site had expanded from a single acre to eight; before the end of the 19th century Woodpecker had been launched; and even before the outbreak of World War II Bulmers was buying up its local competitors. It became the largest cidermaker in the world, churning out industrially-made brands full of chemicals, concentrate and CO_2 for mainly urban markets; however until recently it did produce a traditional draught cider for the region's pubs.

The industrialisation of cider in the Three Counties played an important part in the virtual disappearance of small-scale farm-based production in the second half of the last century. First, Bulmers and others such as Weston's began buying in cider fruit on an advance contract basis. It made more sense for the grower to agree to sell all his output

deep valleys of the Gloucestershire Cotswolds, most of the region is good, rich land – in fact almost all of the Grade I land in the West Midlands, and much of its Grade II land as well, is in central and southern Herefordshire. But rainfall is comparatively high, and much of the soil is heavy red clay; so land uses such as stockrearing and fruit and vegetable growing – not just top fruit but plums, asparagus, soft fruit and, of course, hops – have long predominated over arable.

to the factory for a price agreed in advance than to take his chance on the rise and fall of the market price, so the factories got all the fruit. Consequently, the increasing profitability of cider fruit led to the mechanisation of the business, which meant there were fewer farmworkers to make the cider – and to drink it. So farm-based cidermaking gradually died out as it had in the South West.

Fortunately, independent cidermaking didn't die out altogether. Some of the revivalists, like Dennis Gwatkin of Abbeydore, came of farming stock – Gwatkin picked up the baton his father had dropped a few years earlier. Others, like Ivor and Suzie Dunkerton, could be accurately described as 'Good Lifers' – before coming to Pembridge he had worked in television, she in the theatre. And others, like Mike Henney, come from the mainstream cider industry – he used to work for Bulmers. Today, small independent manufacture in the Three Counties is in the rudest of health.

> The industrialisation of cider in the Three Counties played an important part in the virtual disappearance of small-scale farm-based production in the second half of the last century

Cider fermenting in the barrel at Gwatkins Cider, Herefordshire

Wales

The story of the revival of craft cidermaking in Wales is both remarkable and heartening. That a handful of enthusiasts should not only uncover a moribund tradition and revive it is an example in itself; that they should do so with such stunning success proves that almost anything is possible if you put your whole heart into it.

Historically, the orcharding and cidermaking region that stretches along the Welsh border from Monmouthsire to Radnorshire was more or less an extension of the Three Counties. There's a strong belief that cider was the drink of the Celts long before the Saes (Saxons) arrived; but although there are Welsh place names with an 'apple' element in them (Avalon, the Isle of Apples, is one such), there's no hard evidence that the Ancient Britons actually turned their apples into cider and, given the technological difficulties of making cider, good reason to suppose that they didn't. The fact that there's no Old Welsh word for cider – 'seidr' is a comparatively modern borrowing like 'eglwys' (church) and 'capel' (chapel) and, for that matter, 'ambwlans' (ambulance) – adds weight to the suggestion that the Welsh got their cidermaking from the English.

Be that as it may, by the 19th century many small farmers in the region were making cider and perry (a strong speciality of the district) for their own consumption, to pay wages in, and for barter, just as their neighbours in Herefordshire and Gloucestershire did. Some were growers for the big Herefordshire factories like Symonds and Bulmer's. Enthusiasts have discovered many native Welsh varieties of cider apple and perry pear; and Dave Matthews, founder of Seidr Dai near Cardiff and chairman of the Welsh Perry & Cider Society, has also compiled a fascinating set of interviews with old local farmers who recall making cider – although not for sale – right into the 1960s. But the tradition had virtually died out when Owen Ralph arrived at Old Badlands Farm at Kinnerton, Powys, in 1986 (although even as late as 1998 Dave did hear rumours of a cluster of small farmers still making their own cider around Tredunnock, near Newport).

Owen had previously been farm manager on Bertram Bulmer's estate in Anglesey, where he had made cider for his own consumption. So finding a small orchard of White Norman apples at his new home, he picked up again where he had left off; and as his cider was good, he soon found a market for it.

> The fact that there's no Old Welsh word for cider adds weight to the suggestion that the Welsh got their cidermaking from the English

At about the same time, Troggi Cider was established in Earlswood, Monmouthshire, by Michael Penney; and in the 1990s they were joined by Towy Valley Cider of Carmarthen; Hayward's of Raglan, which won the best cider award at the 1994 Cardiff Beer Festival and then moved to Tregarth in Gwynedd; Black Mountain Cider at Grove Farm, Llanfoist, near Abergavenny; and Rumsey Cider at Gellirhyd Farm near Brecon.

The revival really took off, though, at the turn of the millennium, when by purest coincidence a number of new concerns were launched. In 2000 Dave Matthews and his wife Fiona founded Seidr Dai; Trefor Powell started Seidr ô Sir at Betws Dyserth, Powys, using the produce of an old orchard; and at St Dogmael's, Dyfed, Abbey Cider was set up to use the fruit of even older orchards at the town's Norman abbey.

It gathered pace. Bill George and Drew Gronow founded Gwynt y Ddraig (Dragon's Breath) near Pontypridd in 2001; WM Watkin started making cider from old orchards at Grosmont in 2003; and in 2004 Springfield Cider at Llangovan, Monmouthshire, and Toloja at Lampeter started making cider. Others have since joined them.

The quality of the cider and perry produced by these enthusiastic revivalists is proved by the regularity with which they have appeared among the medallists at CAMRA's National Cider & Perry Awards. Gwynt y Ddraig took silver in the cider competition in 2003 and gold in 2004, and gold in the perry competitions in 2005 and 2006. Owen Ralph won gold in the 2005 cider competition; Blaengawney Cider of Monmouth won bronze in 2008; and Steve Hughes of far-flung Wrexham won the bottled cider competition in 2006.

What drives these revivalists is partly Welsh pride: Toloja, for instance, sells apple and pear juice as well as cider and perry made only from old Welsh varieties in a 100-tree 'museum orchard', and discovering old orchards and old Welsh varieties is a passion for many of the others as well. But it's also that cidermaking is simply a bug that bites, whatever country you make it in. Once it has captured your imagination, it never relaxes its hold.

The South West

Zummerzet is, of course, where the zoider comes from, in popular imagination at least. And indeed Somerset is home to one of Britain's two giant producers: Gaymer's of Attleborough, Norfolk now produce their ciders in Shepton Mallet, since gobbling up many other big names in the industry including Taunton Cider of Taunton and Showering's of Shepton Mallett, also in Somerset; Whiteways of

Whimple, Devon and Coates of Nailsea, Gloucestershire.

Nor is Gaymer's the county's only volume maker: among the region's larger independents Sheppy's of Taunton, and Thatcher's of Sandford near Bristol will be familiar names to supermarket shoppers thanks to their bottled (and, alas, carbonated!) single varietals; Broadoak of Clutton may be a less well-known name but is still a formidable player, producing three-quarters of a million gallons a year even though it was founded only in 1980.

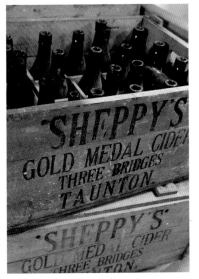

But the glory of the South-West is its plethora of small independents, proud inheritors of the ancient tradition of farm-based cidermaking. In days gone by anyone with enough land to support a few apple trees made cider. Farmers used it to pay their labourers until the Truck Act of 1887 put a stop to the practice; but cottagers made it too, both for their own consumption and for sale, rarely bothering with such niceties as paying duty. As a frustrated Customs official reported in 1830 (five years after the tax on cider had actually been reduced): 'Devon and Somerset are overrun with common sheds by the roadside in which cider is sold in great quantities to people of *both sexes*.' (My italics emphasise the enormity of the crime).

Devon and Somerset are the only counties where the old tradition of cider production as a sideline to livestock rearing has survived more or less unbroken. In a very few cases the art can be traced back literally for centuries: Gray's of Halstow in Devon claims to have been making cider for 300 years, and it is more than likely that there has been cidermaking at Frant's Farm at Dunsford, Somerset, (currently the home of Brimblecombe's cider) for 450 years.

Apple trees in the orchards surrounding the farm at Gray's Devon Cider

Very old Morgan Sweet apple trees in Martin Latimer's orchard, Gloucestershire

Old horse drawn cart, Perry Brothers of Dowlish Wake, Somerset

There are other makers in the region that claim to have been in business for three or four or five generations, stretching back a century or a century and a half, albeit without records to prove their claim. But it's not so much the longevity of a handful of individual producers that proves the strength and vibrancy of the South West's cidermaking tradition as the fact that newcomers constantly emerge here. Perry Brothers of Dowlish Wake, Somerset, for instance, goes back to the 1920s, while Green Valley Cyder of Clyst St George, Devon, was set up only in 1989. Newcomers they may be (in comparative terms, at least), but in many cases they learnt their art at the knee of a veteran, or inherited orchards and presses that were old when they were born. So although their principal consumers nowadays are thirsty tourists rather than thirsty farmhands, they can still claim to be true inheritors of the ancient mantle.

Kent, Sussex & Surrey

Ironic, perhaps, that Kent should be known as the Garden of England when the reason for its long history of growing fruit, vegetables, cobnuts, hops and the like is that its soil and topography make it largely unsuitable for arable. The same might be said for Surrey and Sussex, also historically great places for fruit and, of course, timber, but neither of them noted for cereals.

Still, man does not live by bread alone; and the same soil and topography that made the counties poor in wheat and barley made them rich in apples. Orchard husbandry in the Wealden country is well-attested from the 14th century onwards (even growing vines on the sunnier slopes). Manorial records show the 'great gardens' of all the many castles and, later, country seats well-planted with topfruit of all varieties; and much of it was made into cider. All the Sussex manors of Merton College, Oxford, had cider-presses in the middle ages; and while much of Surrey's chalky soil proved ideal for viticulture, cidermaking was also a great institution in the county.

This was especially so from the late 17th century onwards, when agricultural improvers began to make their presence felt; but perhaps because the nature of farming in the region was so mixed, large-scale industrial cidermaking never emerged here as it did in Herefordshire, Somerset, and to a lesser extent Norfolk. The region's only two sizeable concerns are both comparative newcomers: Merrydown of Horam, Sussex, was founded by two war veterans in 1946 and was originally as well known for its country wines as for its strong ciders; its factory closed in 2004 and in 2005 the business was sold to SHS, proprietor of WKD alcopops among other brands. Still going strong is Biddenden of Biddenden in Kent, founded as a vineyard in 1969 and making light but strong table ciders since 1978.

Nevertheless, the three south-eastern counties are home to a growing band of small makers. Despite the centuries-old tradition of farm cidermaking here, though, it's almost impossible to track down any makers of much antiquity. Double Vision of Boughton Monchelsea, Kent, owes its roots to a long heritage of cidermaking by the Cramp family; it was only founded as a commercial concern, though, in the 1970s. A similar story belongs to Pawley Farm Cider of Faversham, founded in 1979 but claiming to use a family recipe more than two centuries old.

Other than that, the two dozen-odd cidermakers in the region mostly started operations in the 1980s or '90s, often as offshoots of fruit farms or, like Sedlescombe, vineyards. But as they mostly make wonderful cider – Gospel Green and Coldharbour *méthode champenoise* bottled ciders are particularly fine – we shan't hold their youthfulness against them.

East Anglia

Within living memory, huge swathes of Norfolk, Suffolk, Cambridgeshire and Bedfordshire were given over to fruit-growing. Blossom time on the Bedfordshire-Cambridgeshire border, where the Co-op had hundreds of acres of apple and plum orchards, turned the rolling land into a spectacular froth of pink and white flowers. All of that went in the 1970s when the sweeter and cheaper Golden Delicious arrived from France following our accession to the Common Market: orchards were grubbed up wholesale and East Anglia is no longer the fruit-growing region it was.

But East Anglia can claim to be the cradle of English cidermaking, since the art was first officially recorded in Norfolk in 1204 when a tenant in Acle paid as part of his rent a load of pearmains and four hogsheads of the cider made from them.

The Normans brought the words 'pearmain' and 'costard' with them, and presumably also the varieties of apple to which they referred; and apple-growing quickly became a significant part of the East Anglian economy, alongside viticulture. William of Malmesbury, who died in 1143, recorded that the Isle of Ely was so fully cultivated with apples and vineyards that it was like an earthly paradise.

Fruit-growing persisted as a mainstay of farming in all six East Anglian counties until the 1970s. Bedfordshire in the 19th century was the home base of Thomas Laxton, who developed many apple varieties that are with us still; the Warden pear was also developed in the county. Apples, as well as soft fruit, were grown on reclaimed land around Wisbech in Cambridgeshire and in many parts of Essex. Hertfordshire's long tradition of horticulture for the London market included extensive growing of both apples and pears (the Conference pear was first grown here); and both Norfolk and Suffolk were significant producers of all kinds of fruit including apples. Many growers made cider as a sideline, using their surplus cookers and eaters rather than the cider apple varieties grown in the West; a handful still do.

But it was in the 18th century, during the period of agricultural improvement that made the industrial revolution possible, that cidermaking on a commercial scale took off in the region: and two of the great names from the period, Aspall and Gaymer's, are with us still.

Cider fermenting in the barrel at Ross on Wye Cider and Perry

Cidermaking was started at Aspall Hall near Debenham in Suffolk in 1728 when it was bought by a Jerseyman of French Huguenot descent, Clement Chevallier. He first planted vines, but they failed to flourish, so he imported cider-apple trees from his native island instead. The Hall is now in the hands of the eighth generation of the Chevallier family, and the tradition of using cider apples rather than the cookers or eaters more common in the region has also been maintained. The Hall's own orchards are also entirely organic: Perronelle Chevallier Guild, grandmother of the present generation, who died in 2004 aged 102, was a founder member of the Soil Association.

Gaymer's of Attleborough, Norfolk, belongs to the same period of agricultural improvement but now survives, alas, in name only. Robert Gaymer (1738–1821) first made cider at Banham; his son John (1771–1843) married the daughter of Joseph Chapman, author of tracts on agricultural improvement. John's son William (1805–84) installed the company's first hydraulic press at Banham in 1870; and in 1896 William Jnr (1842–1936) moved the company from Banham to Attleborough to be near the railway. Gaymer's Olde English became a national brand, and in 1961 Gaymer's merged with Showering's of Shepton Mallet, Somerset, of Babycham renown. Showering's was taken over by Allied Breweries in 1968, and in 1995 the Attleborough plant was closed and production was transferred to Taunton.

Apart from Aspall, East Anglia still has many small cidermakers including organic pioneer Robbie Crone. But almost without exception they are first-generation newcomers, the tradition of small-scale farm production having been entirely wiped out in the 1970s along with most of the region's commercial orchards.

A golden glass of cider, gloriously sharp and refreshing

VAT N<u>O</u>

Modern cider making equipment at Sheppy's Cider, Tauton, Somerset

People &
Places

Cider People

Traditional cider is glorious stuff, fresh and fruity and full of flavour. The orchards it comes from are glorious places: frothing with blossom in spring, cool and shady in summer, bowed beneath burdens of apples in autumn and site of bucolic rituals in winter. And the people who make it – well, they're a pretty glorious assortment too, from farmers carrying on the work of generations, through newcomers seeking to reconnect with nature and the land, to winemakers who simply want to get more work out of their presses. Some of them are even Benedictine monks!

And to add to the air of mystery that pervades the whole world of cider and cidermakers, nobody knows for sure how many of them there are. HM Customs and Excise doesn't keep a count, because makers of less than 1,500 gallons are exempt from duty. CAMRA's last edition of the *Good Cider Guide*, published in 2005, lists 152; but who can know how many slipped through the net? And how many have started up since then, and how many closed down?

What follows is therefore a crude attempt at a representative cross-section of the people whose toil produces our double-handled mugs of good, wholesome cider and perry. In your journey through the orchards of England and Wales you will meet many more like them, but you will also meet many unlike them – and you will probably, if you are lucky enough, meet some who are quite unlike anyone else at all.

Brimblecombe's Cider

Ron Barter

Farrants Farm, Dunsford, Devon, EX6 7BA
T: 01647 252783

If you're looking for the dim, distant roots of cidermaking in the West Country, then this is the place to search. For it's thought – and on reasonably strong grounds – that cider has been made in the cob barn here since the 17th century.

The barn was originally a Devon longhouse of uncertain date – Tudor or perhaps even medieval – which seems to have been converted into a ciderhouse in the 1600s when the 'new' farmhouse was built. There's a research project here for someone – a postgraduate with a taste for

Ron Barter

The ancient cider press at Brimblecombe's Cider

proper cider could spent an enjoyably hazy two or three years on it – but if the Brimblecombe family tradition is true, this is the oldest continually-working cider house in the country.

Cliff Brimblecombe, now in his 80s, remembers helping to make cider in World War II, but retired in 1996 and sold the land and cider business (the farmhouse was sold separately). The buyer was a neighbouring farmer, Ron Barter, who had moved to Devon to raise cattle after a career as an engineer designing oil rigs and refineries.

'I was based in London and worked all over the world, and I remember thinking, "I can't be doing this when I'm 60",'says Ron. 'When I moved down here I had no great interest in making cider – I was aware of it, of course, and I used to pop into Cliff's for my own supplies; but it wasn't until I heard he was retiring that I decided to buy the business and start making cider myself.'

The farm includes 15 acres of orchards, and Ron buys in extra apples as he needs them; but he stays below the 1,500-gallon duty-exempt limit and runs

beef cattle on the rest of the 130-acre property. He makes cider exactly as Cliff used to, and is one of the few makers still pressing through straw 'cheeses' instead of the more usual nylon hairs. The cider ferments using its own natural yeast for a minimum of five months, but some of it is allowed to mature for far longer – four or five years – in Cognac casks.

'The tannin gives it a little extra bite but it's still very smooth,' says Ron. 'It's fascinating how different vintages mature; the older they get the more distinctive they get, with a lovely long finish.'

Much of the output is sold in the farm shop along with honey, mustard, and other local produce; but Ron enjoys taking it out on the road to sell at food fairs and agricultural shows.

'It gets you out and about, and I love meeting people and explaining to them the difference between commercial brands and the sort of cider I make,' he says. 'I challenge them to taste it, and everyone agrees that mine has far more flavour.'

Old oak barrels in the barn

Burrow Hill Cider & Somerset Cider Brandy Company

Julian Temperley

Pass Vale Farm, Burrow Hill, Kingsbury Episcopi, Somerset, TA12 5BU
T: 01460 240782, www.ciderbrandy.co.uk

Trying to be forward-looking in an industry that trades strongly on its heritage and traditions is no easy task, but in Julian Temperley the world of craft cidermaking has a genuine pioneer who is rooted in its history.

A local lad, Julian had spent some time farming in East Africa – 'chasing cows through the forest' – before coming home and buying Pass Vale some 35 years ago. Then a small mixed farm of 27 acres, it had 10 acres of cider orchards and a cidermaking history going back 150 years.

It was never Julian's plan to start specialising in cider – hardly a logical step, he says, at a time when the tradition of cidermaking for farmworkers was all but dead. But having decided to keep making cider in duty-exempt quantities – 'I grew up drinking cider, and to this day I don't drink beer,' he says – Julian found that it gradually took over the farm... and his life.

He soon started buying more land and planting more orchards, but all the time he was conscious that real cider needed a new direction if it was to survive. The industrial giants were using their tax advantage over beer to create a dumbed-down and largely artificial product firmly aimed at what he describes as 'the yob market'. So Julian decided to do exactly the opposite, and to put fine ciders back where they had been in the 17th and 18th centuries – on the dining tables of the affluent and discerning.

Burrow Hill's smooth and refined ciders – including bottle-fermented versions made by the authentic *méthode Champenoise* – were soon winning awards all over the West Country; but in the mid-1980s Julian went a step further. Bertram Bulmer, *éminence grise* of the Bulmer's dynasty, had fought and won a heroic battle with Customs to establish the King Offa distillery at the Hereford Cider Museum; so Julian and Charles Ponsonby-Fane did exactly the same at Ponsonby-Fane's nearby stately home, Brympton D'Evercy.

That venture was largely educational, says Julian; but a couple of years later he was ready to revive a practice that died out two centuries earlier,

Washing the apples before pressing

and in 1989 he produced his first fully-commercial cider brandy, named Somerset Royal after the apple variety that was its main constituent.

Partly because of its novelty value, partly because of Julian's genius for publicity, and not least because of its quality – smoother and more refined than most Calvados – Somerset Royal Cider Brandy quickly attracted the attention of serious food writers, and thus serious foodies around the world.

Maybe a third of Burrow Hill's output of 150,000 gallons a year now goes to make Somerset Royal Cider Brandy, which is bottled at several ages including the 15-year-old Alchemy, and its brand extensions: Apéritif and Pomona, both blends of brandy and apple juice rather like Pineau des Charentes, and an eau-de-vie flavoured with locally-grown morello cherries.

More recently, though, a dark and heavy storm cloud appeared on Julian's horizon: in redrafting its Wines & Spirits Regulations, the European Commission almost casually struck out the clause permitting the use of the term 'cider brandy', which battling Bertram Bulmer had managed to get inserted nearly 30 years before. Although consulted on the change, the patriotic heroes of the Department for the Environment, Food, & Rural Affairs, always batting for Britain, decided not to demur – and indeed, not even to pass on news of the impending change to Julian.

The regulation came into effect in February 2008, with a 15-month phasing-in period that means that by May this year (2009), it will be illegal to describe anything as brandy unless it is distilled from wine. Julian has, of course, put up a fight, with strong support from the Liberal group in the European Parliament (led, coincidentally, by Julian's local MEP) and, perhaps more surprisingly, the Calvados distillers' association who use the term cider brandy in their biggest export markets. It's now too late to redraft the redrafting of the regulation; but Julian hopes that Protected Geographic Indicator status, for which he has formally applied, will allow him to use the descriptor again. He should know the fate of his application by autumn, which means he faces a minimum of six months' trading using illegal labels. Hopefully no over-zealous trading standards officer will court hatred, ridicule, and contempt by prosecuting him.

Burrow Hill's Somerset Cider Brandy may have found its way onto the dining tables of the affluent and discerning, but once a year it also does its bit to bring real cider to those more used to drinking it over ice. Burrow Hill's cider bus is a regular sight at the nearby Glastonbury Festival – dispensing dry and sweet ciders straight from the barrel to thirsty festivalgoers, as well as their ever popular hot, spiced cider.

If giving birth to, nurturing, and now having to defend his cider brandy seems to dominate Julian's life story, we should not forget that sales of Burrow Hill's fine ciders still tot up to a more-than-respectable 100,000 gallons a year, and Pass Vale Farm has grown over the years from 27 acres to 250 – all, save for a small flock of obliging sheep who keep the grass and brambles down and manure the soil, given over to cider orchards.

Butford Organics

Martin & Janet Harris

Butford Farm, Bowley Lane, Bodenham, Herefordshire, HR1 3LG
T: 01568 797195
www.butfordorganics.co.uk

It's a long step from Leeds to Leominster, but it was one that pensions actuary Martin Harris and his wife Janet, a doctor in the RAF and a Squadron Leader, no less, had long had in mind. For Martin describes himself as an 'ageing hippy' who had only become an actuary because it paid well, but whose real ambition was to have an organic smallholding of his own. Janet felt the same, and when in 1999 the opportunity arose to buy 13 acres in Herefordshire, they took the plunge.

Making cider and perry hadn't been high on the list of activities they planned to pursue; and they started off with a mixture of cattle, pigs, chickens, geese, and arable. They also planted an acre of top fruit, half of it being cider apples.

The mixture proved too rich, though. Cattle were too time-consuming and arable was too capital-intensive. 'You need the same amount of equipment for one acre as you do for 100,' says Martin. In 2004 another opportunity arose, this time to buy a semi-derelict four-acre cider orchard; and with that the focus of the operation changed. The cattle and the arable went, and the herd of pigs was slimmed down to just three. The farm shop, which was opened last year in a renovated barn, still sells pork and eggs and preserves and soft fruit and other produce, but it's the cider and perry that dominates the mix.

'We didn't realise when we started how important the cider was going to become,' says Martin. 'It wasn't high on our agenda, but it's certainly our main enterprise now, especially the perry which is a lot more challenging but is part of the heritage of the region.

We're self-sufficient in apples, having grafted some of the older trees in the orchard to perpetuate the old varieties. But we had one old perry tree which I have budded and planted and we should be self-sufficient in pears as well in five or six years.'

Herefordshire cider orchards

The hard work has certainly paid off in terms of awards: the Harrises' perry won bronze in CAMRA's National Cider and Perry of the Year 2004, and they've also collected gongs at the local Big Apple cider trials and the Three Counties Show. Their speciality is sparkling bottled cider made by the *méthode Normande*, which is a posh way of saying that it's bottled before it's fermented out completely. This is a lot simpler than the *méthode Champenoise* adopted by some bottlers, which involves lots of complicated folderol like *dosage* and *remuage* and *dégorgement* to achieve a naturally sparkling cider

that's drier, but not really any improvement. And anyway, says Martin: 'Our approach to food is to be as non-interventionist as possible.'

Smallholding proved much harder work than the Harrises anticipated, especially as they now have a young family and Janet still works as a GP's locum. But the satisfaction and fulfilment they hoped for is certainly there – especially as they met such a warm welcome from the local cider community.

'Everybody's been incredibly welcoming and supportive and enthusiastic, which is one of the reasons we went into cider,' says Martin.

Crone's Organic Cider

Robbie Crone
Fairview, Fersfield Road, Dam Green, Kenninghall, Norfolk, NR16 2DP
T: 01379 687687
www.crones.co.uk

East Anglia has not exactly been the hotbed of revivalist cidermaking that Herefordshire and Somerset has; but it has its cider heroes, and one of them is undoubtedly Robbie Crone.

Dutch by birth, Robbie came to Norfolk with his mother at the age of 16, and after school embarked on a career first as a restorer of antiques and then as a cabinetmaker. He discovered cidermaking as a hobby when a friend bought an old railway jack from a junkyard and turned it into a rudimentary but perfectly adequate cider press; the bug bit, as it so often does, and by 1988 Robbie had thrown in cabinetmaking and turned full-time cidermaker.

'I liked the cider so much,' he says. 'It was so much better than the commercial fizzy cider which was all I had experienced until then.

And not only was it a wonderful drink, it was an equally wonderful way to make use of all the unwanted apples that were being left to rot in people's gardens and clogging up their lawnmowers. So I started knocking on people's doors and begging to be allowed to scrump their apples, and in the first year I made 150 gallons using my friend's press – and next year I went straight up to 1,500.'

Sourcing fruit on a bigger scale was equally appealing to Robbie's hatred of waste. Commercial growers of organic cookers and eaters had a plentiful supply of apples that were too large or too small or not round enough for the supermarkets but were otherwise perfect: they were only too happy to have a customer to take them off their hands. Robbie only briefly had his own orchard when he bought six acres of trees that were due to be grubbed up, but after three years he found orcharding too expensive and too labour-intensive and sold it on to a grower.

'I'm glad I saved the orchard, but I lost money on it and you'd have to hold a gun to my head to get me to do it again,' he says.

At his peak, Robbie was making 8,000 gallons a year and supplying the Tap & Spile chain of real ale pubs; but the market for his sideline, organic apple juice, was growing and for a while he scaled cider production back to the duty-exempt limit and concentrated on the juice. Then bigger competitors with more money and more marketing muscle got in on the act, and Robbie turned his attention back to cidermaking.

'Besides,' he says, 'apple juice is boring.'

In 2007, Robbie made around 6,000 gallons using cookers and eaters – 'but not too many Bramleys, mind' – with a small admixture of cider apples imported from Wiltshire for tannic bite. He was planning to increase output further in 2008 and says he can sell all he can make without too much effort, partly because of his organic status. Most of his production is bottled and goes to specialist off-licences or via organic wholesalers to wholefood shops, but he also delivers five-gallon polycasks to pubs throughout East Anglia. 'In the old days I used to deliver as far afield as Manchester and Morpeth, but I don't have to do that any more,' he says.

Hecks
Farmhouse Cider

John Heck
9-11 Middle Leigh, Street, Somerset BA16 0LB
T: 01458 442367
www.hecksfarmhousecider.co.uk

John Heck was born on the edge of the Somerset village of Street, in the shadow of Glastonbury Tor, over 70 years ago and now lives almost in the middle of it. Not that he's moved; but the village has expanded over the years until the small family farm and its shop is almost surrounded. In fact the Heck family hasn't gone anywhere since 1897, when they arrived at Middle Leigh from Chard, where their records show they had been making cider since at least 1841.

That makes John the fifth generation cidermaker in the Heck family; and unlike many other family concerns the next generation – Andrew and

Andrew and Chris Heck

Chris – have decided to keep the tradition going. John, who took over the business when his father died over 50 years ago, has handed on the baton to his sons but continues to help out. 'I'm supposed to be retired, but it's hard not to stay involved when you live on the premises,' he says.

That Andrew and Chris have embraced the family business isn't the only untypical thing about Hecks. For one thing, the family isn't afraid to keep up with modern methods. John can just remember the old mill, which was driven by a petrol engine, and the old hand-turned twin-screw press; but his father replaced them with hydraulic equipment in 1939. A brand-new belt-press was installed only four years ago, and the harvesting is also done mechanically these days.

'And a good thing too,' John agrees. 'You wouldn't believe how cold it could be picking apples by hand – I think the winters must've been colder in the old days!'

For another, Hecks makes perry – rare enough in the Three Counties; even more so in Somerset.

Suitable fruit is, as elsewhere, hard to come by, but, says John: 'We've planted quite a few trees ourselves over the years, and there are one or two other orchards around here.' He was looking forward to a fair crop in 2008, so there should be enough for all.

Yet a third untypical thing about Hecks is that at a time when many other traditional cidermakers have been feeling the pinch, business at Middle Leigh is good. Production has increased from around 10,000 gallons a year in the mid-1990s to 20-25,000 gallons now, and the family has bought several small orchards in the area to keep up with demand. The Hecks now have about 15 acres of their own, including a patch in Compton Dando that has been a cider orchard since 1760. They also buy fruit from local farmers, which has prevented the grubbing out of many small orchards over the years; and they've stopped growing strawberries because cidermaking is more profitable.

'The Magners effect has actually helped us,' says John. 'More people are drinking cider these days, and when they try ours – although it's nothing like Magners! – they find they like it.' Trade in the shop, which also sells local produce such as honey, mustard, apple juice (Hecks makes 18 varieties, including Cox's as well as cider apple juice) and Julian Temperley's Somerset Royal cider brandy, has been helped by the erection of brown tourist signs, which divert a stream of tourists from the dubious glories of The Village, a nightmarish retail park on the site of the old Clarks shoe factory. 'They were difficult enough to get approval for, but they've been well worth the effort,' says John. Then there are 'exports' via wholesalers to CAMRA festivals all over the country; and there are still a fair number of pubs in the district that buy the draught product.

So it's pleasing to be able to say that all's well that ends well – or in Hecks Farmhouse Cider's case, all's well that carries on well.

Old oak barrels storing cider at Hecks Farmhouse Cider

Minchew's Real Cyder & Perry

Kevin Minchew

Rose Cottage, Aston Cross, Tewkesbury, Gloucestershire, GL20 8HX
T: 01684 773427
www.minchews.co.uk

Born on a smallholding in Ashchurch near Tewkesbury, Kevin Minchew remembers somewhat reluctantly helping his father pick fruit from the orchard to make cider and perry. There was always a barrel on the go in the stable, he recalls; but while cider was the everyday drink for family and visitors, the perry was kept for special occasions.

Although he considered helping out a bit of a chore, the smell of the perry pears in their hessian sacks never left his nostrils. 'Even today that autumnal scent floods me with memories of the pear orchards, whose immense trunks and canopies brought out an almost religious awe similar to the feeling one gets among the columns of churches and cathedrals,' he says.

As a teenager, Kevin started frequenting the ciderhouses that still dotted the area around Bredon Hill, and in 1984 he started making cider and perry as a hobby. After a few years he

Kevin Minchew

The Gloucestershire orchard where Minchew's source their cider apples

decided to take a course in cidermaking at Hindlip College in Pershore, and in 1993, when one of his early attempts won the annual cider competition held at Putley Village Hall in Herefordshire, he launched himself into the world of commerce as Minchew's Real Cyder & Perry.

As the majestic pear orchards he remembered from his childhood had mostly been grubbed out by then, he started scouring the hedgerows and cottage gardens of the Three Counties to rescue specimens of now-rare varieties and became an expert in the arcane mysteries of grafting and budding, planting new perry pear trees in friends' gardens and any patches of land he could find. Later, and with the collaboration of a group of like-minded enthusiasts, this developed into an officially recognised National Collection, planted at the Three Counties Showground at Malvern where to this day dozens of specimen trees are available to act as the foundations of new perry orchards. (The one variety that has eluded him is the legendary Late Treacle,

last seen in 1963, and still something of a Holy Grail for amateur pomologists).

The 1990s were something of a boom time for traditional cider; but like many small-scale makers Kevin has felt the squeeze as the retail trade becomes increasingly concentrated. The number of pubs stocking independently-made cider is shrinking, while supermarkets have taken over from the local shops that used to sell Kevin's cider and perry. On top of that, fruit-pickers are harder to recruit, so Kevin now only makes the duty-exempt 1,500 gallons a year.

'Some of the independents have opted to expand, but they mostly have their own orchards and shops which I don't,' he says. 'Times are certainly harder than they were 10 years ago.'

But even though his output is limited, the range of his products is, he thinks, unequalled at some two dozen bottled single-varietal ciders and perries. So although Minchew's Real Cyder & Perry is not exactly big business, Kevin can be justly proud as his reputation as one of the saviours of perry.

Sedlescombe
Organic Vineyard

SOIL ASSOCIATION · ORGANIC STANDARD ·

Roy Cook

**Hawkshurst Road, Cripps Corner, Robertsbridge,
East Sussex, TN32 5SA
T: 01580 830715**
www.englishorganicwine.co.uk

Growing grapes and making wine can be a chancy business in the British climate, and many English and Welsh winemakers have found a good sideline in utilising the more reliable apple crop. The technologies are similar, and the apple harvest fits neatly round the grape harvest. Biddenden in Kent, Shawsgate in Suffolk, and Porthallow in Cornwall were among those that came to making cider via making wine; and so was England's oldest organic vineyard.

Sedlescombe was founded in 1979 by Roy Cook, who was teaching English in Germany when he was left 10 acres of land in East Sussex. He knew that such a small plot would have to be worked pretty intensively to yield a worthwhile income, and his first thought was growing salad veg in polytunnels. But the plot was south-facing and well-drained, so he thought he'd have a crack at growing grapes instead.

Not that he was inspired by any knowledge of the German wine industry: he worked in Karlsrühe, which is south of the Palatinate wine region and west of Franconia (well-known for its apple wines as well as the grape variety) so he had no personal contact with winemakers. But his fluency in German did come in handy. 'Speaking German did mean I could read all the German winemaking manuals,' he says.

As luck would have it, the orchards just across the road from Roy's vineyard were on land surrounding a Southern Water reservoir; and in the 1980s it was decided to go organic in order to eliminate the run-off of pesticides and fertilisers into the water. Cidermaking would add a second string to his financial bow, Roy reckoned, and a steady source of organic apples so close at hand was too good a chance to pass up. So he put in a bid for all the undersized and misshapen fruit that the supermarkets would reject, installed a mill and press, and has never looked back. Southern Water has since sold the orchards to the man who used to manage them, Eric Rowland, who supplies Tesco and still lets Roy have the apples Tesco won't accept.

Roy's cider, like many easterners, is made from sweet dessert apples for alcohol with Bramleys for acidity. The alcohol content is regulated with an addition of sugar; and more sugar is added at the bottling stage for body. The cider is pasteurised, but other than that it's entirely natural: all juice, and fermented to dryness with naturally-occurring yeast.

For a few years in the late 1990s Sedlescombe cider was listed by Waitrose; but other than that it has always been a sideline.

'It evens things out in a bad year,' says Roy. 'In 2007 the heavy spring rain meant the fruit never set on the vines, and the crop was down to 10% of its usual yield. The cider was very useful then, but usually I'll only make 400 gallons or so.'

Now that Waitrose has decided it can do without Roy's cider, the best places to find it are in local farmers' markets or in Sedlescombe's own shop. The shop is open from 10.30-5.00 every day from Easter to Christmas, and Sedlescombe also has a pleasant nature trail through its two acres of woodland that attracts 4-5,000 visitors a year.

Collecting perry pears for
Kevin Minchew's perry
production, Gloucestershire

Steve Hughes

Dafarn Dywyrch Farm, Llandegla, Wrexham, Clwyd
T: 01978 790650/222

Wherever you can grow apples, you can make cider – even if you're 1,000ft up in the hills of North Wales. And not just any old cider, either, but a cider good enough to win a national award.

Actually, it was a bit embarrassing for Steve Hughes, who won CAMRA's Bottled Cider Award in 2006 with the very first batch he'd ever made. The organisers rang to tell him he'd won and ask for 200 bottles to sell on the cider bar at the Great British Beer Festival. Unfortunately he'd only made five gallons and just had 12 bottles left, which he'd rather hoped to keep for himself.

Steve's family have been farming at Dafarn Dywyrch for at least 200 years. At one time it was a pub that brewed its own ale as well as a farm – George Borrow recalled in his book *Wild Wales*, written in the 1860s, that he'd been refused a pint there for being an Englishman who presumed to speak Welsh. But cider? Not until 2005.

That was when Steve – who works in a local factory while dad Jim runs the farm – started making cider as a hobby. As a schoolboy he'd relied on a diet of Woodpecker Cider and Murray Mints to help him revise for his exams, and he'd also been a home winemaker. He was inspired to try his hand at cider when he saw Owen Ralph give a demonstration of pressing at an open day at Erddig Hall. So he ordered 20 cider apple trees and planted them, despite being more than twice the recommended altitude; and while he was waiting for them to bear he made cider from local fruit, including crab apples and an unidentified wilding he found growing in a pub car park.

The cider that won the following year's competition was milled with a pick handle in a galvanised bucket and pressed on a homemade contraption of Steve's own devising. But victory inspired him to take things a step further. He found an ancient Herefordshire twin-screw press at a steam fair and picked up an equally derelict scratter mill in Worcestershire, restored them himself, and carried on planting more

Old Gloucestershire cider orchard

trees. That autumn he made 700 gallons, entering the 2007 Bath & West Show and winning bronze there. That autumn, in turn, he made 3,000 gallons, taking a brave step beyond the 1,500-gallon duty-exempt limit; for although he still works in the factory, he aims to make a full-time business of his cider – and as he also has an MBA, he stands every chance of success.

But if growing cider apple trees in North Wales is tough – the most successful varieties come from Gloucestershire, says Steve, which like Llandegla has thin soil over limestone; but even so they only yield a third of what you'd expect – selling the cider is tougher still. This is a region with no cider tradition at all, and Steve is having to carve out a niche not just for his own product but for the whole idea of strong, still, West Country-style cider.

> **Steve Hughes won CAMRA's Bottled Cider Award in 2006 with the very first batch he'd ever made**

About a third of his sales are 'exported' – whisked away by a wholesaler to sell mainly at festivals. Another third of sales are of Bottled Rosie's Triple D (named after his dog) and Wicked Wasp (named after the wasp that stung him as he was giving a pressing demonstration at a steam fair), mainly through farmers' markets and a few local shops. The final third is in bag-in-box to local pubs. 'I think at first they thought they were doing me a favour by taking some of my cider,' he says. 'But now it's getting a reputation and I'm beginning to get repeat orders.'

The next step for Steve, ever-ambitious, is to grow the business and give up the day job – and that means a licensed shop at Dafarn Dywyrch.

'We're at one end of the Horseshoe Pass so we have streams of tourists passing by,' he says. 'It's just a question of picking the right moment.'

Whin Hill Cider

Pete Lynn & Jim Fergusson
The Stables, Stearmans Yard, Wells-next-the-Sea, Norfolk, NR23 1BW
T: 01328 711033
www.whinhillcider.co.uk

Traditionally, cider in East Anglia is supposed to be made from cookers and eaters rather than the specialised cider varieties you find in the west. But not at Whin Hill.

Friends for many years, Pete Lynn and Jim Fergusson had met at a pub in Norwich and both liked a drop of cider – so much so that they eventually started making their own as a hobby on a hand-cranked basket-press. A few years down the line, Pete had become a water board

engineer and Jim was working for the electricity board but, says Jim: 'We couldn't see ourselves doing that for the rest of our lives.'

The decision to start making cider for a living wasn't based on local tradition: Jim and Pete didn't know of any old-established cider barns where they could sit around quaffing scrumpy with ancient yokels who'd been at it for generations. They just thought they'd spotted a gap in the market that seemed to offer a good business and a pleasing change of lifestyle; so in 1994 they bought 16 acres of farmland and planted it up with proper cider apple and perry pear trees imported from the West Country. 'We just preferred the West Country taste,' says Jim. And to those chauvinistic westerners who say you can't grow cider apple trees in the more arid climate of East Anglia, Pete and Jim's answer is: 'Yes we can'. They had to import cider apples from the west while their own orchard was getting established but now, says Jim, they're self-sufficient in fruit and can make 7-8,000 gallons in a good year.

The cider is milled and pressed at the orchard, on second-hand but modern equipment, but the place to get your Whin Hill cider is the partners' own shop in Wells-next-the-Sea, which they moved into in 1998 and where they also sell apple juice, cider vinegar, honey, and beer from local small independent brewers. It's open from 10.30-5.30 at weekends from Easter to October, and in the July-August peak it's open every day except Monday. It's also where the cider is fermented and bottled, although the ancient mill and double-screw press are just for show.

And the ciders themselves? They do dry and medium still blends, medium and sweet sparkling blends; a perry from their own trees; an extra-dry bottle-fermented cider; a still special blend made from the pick of the crop; and Major, Brown's, and Dabinett single-varietals.

Roger Wilkins' old cider orchards, overlooking the Somerset Levels

Wilkins Cider

Roger Wilkins

Land's End Farm, Mudgley, Wedmore, Somerset, BS28 4TU
T: 01934 712385

Undoubtedly one of the Grand Masters of absolutely traditional Somerset cidermaking, Roger Wilkins has been drinking cider since he was five – and now he's 61.

Roger's grandfather started making cider at Land's End Farm in 1918, and taught him how to make it in exactly the same way. In those days, Roger recalls, most local farmers still made their own cider – seven of them along a two-mile stretch of his road alone. But an awful lot has changed since those heady days.

Roger took over running the business in the 1960s, when he was scarcely 20 years old. At that time the farm was turning out some 5,000 gallons a year, much of it for sale to local pubs. Then in 1976 came Dennis Healey's decision to tax farm cider, and Roger had a big decision to make: retreat, as so many others did, to below the 1,500-gallon tax-exempt limit; or expand.

'It wasn't worth staying at 5,000 gallons – the tax would have taken all the profit,' he says. So he expanded. It proved a wise decision – in 1982, his best year, he made 80,000 gallons. But the drink-drive limit, changing tastes among the younger local drinkers, and the purchase of free houses by breweries and pub companies gradually eroded the market for the traditional product and by the early years of this century Roger's output was down to 10,000 gallons. He had also stopped making perry.

'Those breweries, they don't care what the landlord wants and they don't care what the customer wants,' he says. 'They tie them for everything because all they want is their money.'

But what goes around comes around, and output is creeping up again at Land's End Farm – mainly, says Roger, because a new generation is discovering traditional cider.

'It's not the same sort of quantities as in the old days, mind,' he says. 'A pub would take five gallons at a time, while the people who come

Apples ready to be loaded on the 'elevator'

The tap room

to the farm shop will buy half a gallon or maybe a gallon at most. It takes a lot of shop sales to make up for all those pubs.'

Roger still delivers within 15 miles; wholesalers take a fair amount off him; and his shop does a brisk business in farmhouse cheese and other local produce as well as cider – and perry. In the last couple of years he's started making it again – although only 3-400 gallons a year. 'Perry pears are hard to come by; you have to go to Herefordshire or Gloucestershire to get them really,' he says.

As you'd expect, everything about Roger's cider is absolutely natural, right down to the yeast, and all of it is fermented to dryness. To make sweet cider, Roger adds a teaspoon of saccharine for each 20 gallons; to make medium, he blends dry and sweet. But it's made in the old-fashioned way, all blended and none of your new-fangled single varietals, fermented and ready to drink in only 8-10 weeks rather than the five months that some ciders take. Roger says that that's how it used to be done when

farmworkers liked their cider 'a bit rough'. (Well, let's say 'fresh'). The perry is made with an admixture of 10% apple juice because, he says, the pear's own yeast is slower to work than the apple's, and he likes his perry to be ready by Christmas.

With his roots planted firmly in the Somerset soil, Roger is just a little bit scornful of the newcomers to cidermaking in the county. 'It's not something you can learn at college,' he says. 'You have to learn it by doing it over the years. I don't test for acidity and gravity and that sort of thing – I've been drinking cider since I was five and I know how it ought to taste. I do everything by taste, including the blend.

Why test it if you can taste it?'

Roger Wilkins (right) and fellow cider makers

Where to drink Cider

Traditional cider and perry account for only 5-10% of the national cider market, and outside the South-West and the Three Counties they're regrettably hard to find. Of course, if you happen to find yourself in Cornwall, Devon, Somerset or Herefordshire, virtually every grocer and gift-shop will sell you local scrumpy, often in unappealing plastic jerrycans and often at an unappealing price. But elsewhere in Britain, you have to know where to look.

And where there's a will there's a way. All the major supermarket chains stock bottled single-varietals from the likes of Thatcher's, Sheppy's, Dunkerton's and Henney's, and even though they're invariably carbonated they're not a bad substitute. A few brands of proper still cider are nationally distributed: some supermarket chains carry 3-litre bag-in-boxes from Weston's, and the Co-op has its own-label bottled still cider: Tillington Hills Dry Reserve, made of apples from its last surviving orchards just north of Hereford. These only escaped the bulldozer when the Co-op grubbed up its orchards in the rest of the country because the land here isn't suitable for arable; for years the fruit has been sold to Bulmer's, but now the Co-op very sensibly sends a certain proportion to Knight's of Storridge to be made into a more than passable table cider of 6% alcohol by volume. If your local branch doesn't stock it, corner the manager and insist!

Other than that, let CAMRA be your friend. The Good Beer Guide includes some 5,000 excellent real ale pubs, and those that stock real cider are marked out by a little apple in the symbols that detail the facilities of each entry. There's a surprising number of them, too: to pick a few of the unlikelier counties, 14 are listed each for Merseyside and South Yorkshire; County Durham has nine; and even the Highlands & Islands has six. (The 650-odd pubs in the JD Wetherspoon chain also have the option to stock real draught cider from Weston's: if your local Wetherspoon doesn't, then as with the Co-op, corner the manager and accept no excuses).

The cider and perry bar at the Great British Beer Festival

Then there are CAMRA beer festivals. The Great British Beer Festival, held at Earl's Court in the first week of August every year, has a massive cider and perry bar, staffed by enthusiastic experts who happily guide novices towards a suitable choice; and it's a real eye-opener to see the delighted expressions on the faces of festivalgoers who've just experienced real perry for the first time.

Some regional festivals, such as the one in Cardiff, have even changed their name to Beer & Cider Festival; and the National Cider & Perry of the Year competition is hosted by Reading Beer Festival every May, when the new season's cider is ready.

Alas, though, your local CAMRA beer (and cider!) festival comes but once a year; so bring along a few containers and stock up!

CAMPAIGN FOR REAL ALE

Cider Festivals

The Campaign for Real Ale's beer and cider festivals give drinkers all over the country the chance to try real cider and perry. This list gives an overview of the CAMRA festivals that regularly serve real cider and perry, but there is no guarantee that these festivals will be occurring on an annual basis. For up-to-date information check the beer festivals section on the CAMRA website: www.camra.org.uk

January

Cambridge Winter Ale Festival
Colchester Winter Ale Festival
Derby Twelfth Night Winter Beer Festival
Exeter Festival of Winter Ales
Manchester National Winter Ales Festival

February

Battersea Beer Festival
Bodmin Beer Festival
Bradford Beer Festival
Chelmsford Winter Beer Festival
Chesterfield CAMRA Beer Festival
Dorchester Beer Festival
Fleetwood Beer Festival
Gosport Winterfest
Liverpool Beer Festival
Luton Beer Festival
Pendle Beer Festival
Rotherham Oakwood Legendary Real Ale Festival

Stockton Ale & Arty
Tewkesbury Winter Ales Festival

March

Bexley Beer Festival
Bradford Beer Festival
Bristol Beer Festival
Burton Spring Beer & Cider Festival
Darlington Spring Thing
Ely Elysian Beer Festival
Hitchin Beer & Cider Festival
Hove Sussex Beer & Cider Festival
Hull Real Ale & Cider Festival
Leeds Beer, Cider & Perry Festival
Leicester Beer Festival
London London Drinker Beer & Cider Festival
Loughborough Beer Festival
Oldham Beer Festival
Overton (Hants) Beer Festival
St Neots Beer Festival
Walsall Beer Festival
Winslow Beer Festival

April

Bury St Edmunds East Anglian Beer Festival
Chippenham Beer Festival
Coventry Beer Festival
Doncaster Beer Festival
Farnham Beer Festival
Maldon Beer Festival
Mansfield Beer & Cider Festival
Newcastle-upon-Tyne Beer Festival
Paisley Beer Festival
Thanet Easter Beer Festival

May

Alloa Beer Festival
Banbury Beer Festival
Barrow Hill Rail Ale
Cambridge Beer Festival
Chester Charity Beer Festival
Colchester Real Ale & Cider Festival
Glenrothes Kingdom of Fife Beer Festival
Halifax Mayfest
Ilkeston, Erewash Valley Beer Festival
Lincoln Beer Festival
Macclesfield Beer Festival
Newark Beer Festival
Northampton, Delapre Abbey Beer Festival
Reading Beer & Cider Festival
Rugby Beer Festival
Skipton Beer Festival
Stockport Beer & Cider Festival
Stourbridge Beer Festival
Stratford-upon-Avon Beer & Cider Festival
Wolverhampton Beer Festival
Yapton Beerex

June

Aberdeen Great Grampian Beer Festival
Braintree Real Ale Festival
Cardiff Great Welsh Beer & Cider Festival
Edinburgh Scottish Real Ale Festival
Kingston-upon-Thames Beer Festival
Lewes South Downs Beer & Cider Festival
Southampton Beer Festival
St Ives (Cornwall) Beer Festival
Stafford Real Ale Festival
Thurrock Beer Festival
Woodchurch Rare Breeds Beer Festival

July

Ardingly Beer Festival
Boxmoor Beer Festival
Bromsgrove Beer Festival
Canterbury Kent Beer Festival
Chelmsford Beer Festival
Devizes Beer Festival
Ealing Beer Festival
Greenwich Beer & Jazz Festival
Hereford, Beer on the Wye
Plymouth Beer Festival
Winchcombe Cotswold Beer Festival
Woodcote Festival of Ales

August

Boston Steam & Vintage Festival
Clacton-on-Sea Beer Festival
Durham Beer Festival
Grantham Summer Beer Festival
Harbury Beer Festival
London Great British Beer Festival
Peterborough Beer Festival
South Shields Beer Festival
Swansea Beer Festival
Worcester Beer & Cider Festival

September

Ascot Racecourse Beer Festival
Birmingham Beer Festival
Bridgenorth Severn Valley Beer Festival
Burton Beer Festival
Camarthen Beer Festival
Chappel Beer Festival
Chester Autumn Beer Festival
Darlington Rhythm 'N' Brews Beer Festival
Glossop Beer & Cider Festival
Hinckley Beer Festival
Ipswich Beer Festival
Jersey Beer & Cider Festival
Keighley Beer, Cider & Perry Festival
Letchworth Garden City Beer & Cider Festival
Lytham Beer Festival
Maidstone Beer Festival
Melton Mowbray Beer Festival
Minehead Somerset Beer Festival
Moreton-in-Marsh North Cotswold Beer Festival
Nantwich Beer Festival
Newton Abbot South Devon Beer Festival
Rochford Cider & Perry Festival
Shrewsbury Real Ale Festival
Southport Sandgrounder Beer Festival
St Albans Beer Festival
St Ives (Cambs) Booze On The Ouse
Tamworth Beer Festival
Ulverston Charter Beer Festival

October

Barnsley Beer & Cider Festival
Basingstoke Beer Festival
Bedford Beer & Cider Festival
Chester Autumn Beer Festival
Falmouth Beer Festival
Huddersfield Oktoberfest Beer & Cider Festival
Louth Louth & District Beer Festival
Norwich Beer Festival
Nottingham Robin Hood Beer Festival
Poole Beer Festival
Redhill Beer Festival
Richmond (N Yorks) Ale Festival
Sheffield Steel City Beer & Cider Festival
Solihull Beer Festival
Stoke-on-Trent Beer Festival
Thanet Cider Festival
Troon Ayrshire Real Ale Festival
Twickenham Beer & Cider Festival,
Wallington Croydon & Sutton Real Ale & Cider Festival
Weymouth Octoberfest
Worthing Beer Festival

November

Stoke Beer Festival
Watford Beer Festival
Whitchurch (Hants) Beer Festival

December

Hackney Pig's Ear Beer & Cider Festival
Harwich Winter Ale Festival

Cider Houses

Cider houses that sold little or ·
no beer were until comparatively
recently fairly commonplace in
many western and south-western
counties. Some of them even made
their own cider. From the 1960s,
though, they started to close along
with so many other marginally-
profitable little country pubs,
many of which had been run on a
part-time basis. In fact it was the
closure of his local cider house
that prompted Kevin Minchew to start making his own cider and led, by
stages, to the saving of so many rare perry pear varieties from extinction.

There are, however, a handful of surviving cider houses; and listed here
are some of the better ones we know, along with one newcomer.

Bristol & Exeter Inn
135 St John St, Bridgwater, Somerset, TA6 5JA
T: 01278 423722
One-room traditional backstreet boozer 150 yards from the town's
station: the pub's name refers to the old railway line before it was taken
over by the Great Western.

The B&E is not a true cider house in that it sells no beer at all: keg
John Smith's and Bass satisfy the needs of the beerdrinkers here. But it
is as it has been for many, many years, a pub where cider rules. Not that
being a cider house isn't without its problems: owner John Wootten has
been through several changes of supplier in recent years as Lane's went
out of business, Coombes sold up, and Thatcher's started charging a
£12 deposit (+ VAT) on polybarrels. John has now settled on Rich's, and
there's nothing wrong with that.

Top and left: The Cider House, Woodmancote, and proprietor Graham Collins

Inside of the Cider House, Woodmancote, Worcestershire

The Cider Centre
Brandy Wharf, Waddingham,
Lincolnshire, DN21 4RU
T: 01652 678364

Enjoying a glorious setting beside the broad River Ancholme, Brandy Wharf was an ordinary little country pub until 1986 when the then owners, Ian and Gillian Horsley, inspired by a trip to Somerset, decided to stop selling beer and concentrate on cider instead. It was pretty much a whim – there's no tradition of cidermaking in these parts – but it paid off.

The uniqueness, combined with the setting and a food offering that included scrumpy sausages, made Brandy Wharf enormously popular with people from nearby towns such as Scunthorpe, Grimsby and Lincoln. Just as well, really, as hardly anyone lives within walking distance and on a miserable day the pub can go without custom altogether.

The Horsleys sold up in 2002 and the new owners, David and Catherine Wells, have broken with tradition only to the extent of adding Foster's lager to the drinks menu. Other than that they have 12-15 ciders on draught (including some keg), drawn mainly from the Weston's range but including guests from the likes of Perry Brothers, Cheddar Valley, Thatcher's and Banham.

The Cider House
(aka the Monkey House)
Woodmancote, Defford, Worcestershire
T: 01386 750234

Surely one of the oddest pubs in the country. The house itself isn't even licensed; the 'pub' comprises only the garden and the tiny old bakehouse, which is warmed in winter with a little woodburning stove.

Above and below: The Cider House in Wootton Green, Quatt, Shropshire

Woodmancote cider used to be made specially for the pub by Bulmer's; when Bulmer's stopped making traditional cider Weston's took up the baton, and the pub also now sells Weston's First Quality Cider and Country Perry. Other than that, there's only wine, soft drinks, and crisps and peanuts; but customers are welcome to bring their own food and many of them do.

Sadly, custom has been hard hit by the soaring cost of petrol; and as proprietors Graham and Jill Collins are both approaching retirement age they have decided to restrict their opening hours to Friday-Monday lunchtimes and Wednesday-Saturday evenings.

The Cider House

Wootton Green, Quatt, Shropshire, WW15 6EB T: 01746 780285.

Once a smallholding with its own orchard (now a large car park) and its own cider press, the Cider House has stocked a full range – including keg –

from Weston's since Bulmer's gave up on real cider a few years ago. It's also possibly unique in having Somerset Royal Cider Brandy on Optic, but there's no wine or beer. Food is generally restricted to filled rolls, but in good weather the pub holds well-attended barbecues.

Although it's tucked away in some of the prettiest countryside in the county, the owners are keen to stress that it's not remote and not hard to find – in fact it's a mere half-a-mile off the A458 Bridgnorth-Stourbridge road.

Ralph's Cider & Perry

Old Badland, New Radnor, Powys, LD8 2TG
T: 01544 350304

A welcome addition to the short roll-call of cider houses is Ty Bach Seidr at Owen Ralph's cider farm in Radnorshire.

Owen started making cider in 1976, taking up where his grandfather had left off. He moved to Old Badland in 1986 and found there an ancient orchard of White Norman apples, which he pressed into service at first for his own private delectation, but from 1997 as a fully commercial venture. But despite the growing popularity of his cider at farmers' markets and in farm shops, he couldn't get many pubs to stock it. So he opened his own.

Ty Bach Seidr is a converted and extended store-room and outside privy at Old Badland (hence the name, Ty Bach being Welsh for the smallest room) where Ralph's ciders and perries are for sale from oak barrels, either to drink then and there or to take home. The décor majors on a collection of old cider dripmats and bar towels, and there's plenty of exposed beams and bare brick to create the correct atmosphere for the genre. A worthy addition to the stock.

Ye Olde Cider Bar

99 East Street, Newton Abbot, Devon, TQ12 2LD
T: 01626 354221

An absolute gem which has been run by the same landlord, Richard Knibbs, for some 40 years. Sells up to a dozen draught real ciders and perries, all dispensed straight from barrels mounted behind the bar, plus even more in bottle. There's also a range of country wines – but no beer or spirits. Food is limited to local pasties and pies.

Right: Ye Olde Cider Bar, Newton Abbot, Devon

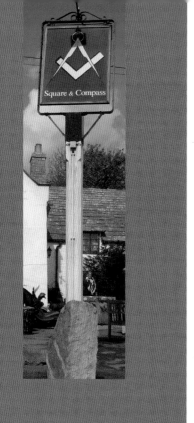

Cider *Pub* of the *Year* *Winners*

Traditional still draught cider and perry used to be surprisingly common in pubs and clubs in many parts of the country, not just in rural Somerset and Devon but also in the industrial towns and cities of South-West England and South Wales where Bulmer's and Taunton were still promoting their versions. But in the early years of this century the big boys abandoned the traditional cider market, and although Weston's and Thatcher's were there to plug the gap, traditional draught cider suffered a heavy blow.

At the same time, traditional draught ciders from small independent makers were getting harder to find even in their home regions. While the older cider-drinkers were, quite literally, dying off, younger drinkers increasingly preferred the heavily-advertised national keg brands, or, worse still, were being seduced by lagers and alcopops.

This was the background against which CAMRA decided, in 2004, to launch a National Cider Pub of the Year competition. The National Cider & Perry Competition had been going for many years, and had recently been joined by the Pomona Award for the person, institution or organisation that had done most during the year to promote traditional cider and perry. But it was felt that a high-profile award scheme specifically for pubs would

Kevin Hunt and Charlie Newman

raise the profile of real cider in the on-licensed trade and encourage more licensees to stock it.

Here are the winners and runners-up so far: the best way to salute their achievement is to visit their pubs and down a pint or three.

Inside the Square & Compass

Peaceful view from outside the Square & Compass

2008

Square & Compass
Worth Matravers, Dorset, BH19 3LF
T: 01929 439229

Twice a runner-up in this competition, the Square and Compass impressed the CAMRA judges enough to earn top spot in 2008.

It's not just its cider and perry that make this pub worth seeking out – the Square and Compass is one of only nine pubs in the UK to have featured in all 36 editions of the CAMRA *Good Beer Guide*, meaning that its beer is something special too. This is a perfect example of a pub that has thrived due to a great variety of locally-sourced produce, and a continual commitment to diversity, which is obvious by its extensive array at the bar.

The Square and Compass boasts a rich family history, having been owned by the same family for several generations. Perched on Dorset's Jurassic coast, overlooking the sea, much of the pub garden furniture is made from driftwood, adding to its uniqueness and earning it one judge's description as 'a characterful pub with beautiful vistas over the channel and an excellent array of cider and perry.'

Runners up:

Coopers Tavern
43 Cross Street, Burton-upon-Trent, Staffordshire, DE14 1EG
T: 01283 532551

Odd one Out
28 Mersea Road, Colchster, Essex, CO2 7ET
T: 01206 578140

Valley Bar
See p108

2007

Valley Bar

51 Valley Rd, Scarborough, Yorkshire, YO11 2LX
T: 01723 372593
www.valleypublichouse.co.uk

The Valley, like the previous year's winner, is in a part of England not known for its ciders. And, again like the 2006 winner, real cider and perry had only been introduced to the pub two years previously.

The Valley was John and Linda Soden's first pub, and though they were ale enthusiasts they only found out about real cider when they decided to stock some at one of their regular beer festivals. It was the start of something big: they now regularly have six to eight real draught ciders, constantly changing, from all over the country, and Linda believes that 85% of her regulars – including confirmed lager drinkers – include real cider in their drinking repertoires.

The Valley also has seven real ales, 100 Belgian beers, a dining room, and B&B. So if you're thinking of a break in Scarborough – and you should – it would be folly to stay anywhere else.

Runners up:

Bell Inn
Bulmore Road, Caerleon, Monmouthshire, NP18 1QQ
T: 01633 420613
www.thebellatcaerleon.co.uk

Pembury Tavern
90 Amhurst Road, Hackney, London, E8 1JH
T: 020 8986 8597
www.individualpubs.co.uk

Square & Compass
See p107

2006

Old Poets' Corner

Butts Rd, Ashover, Derbyshire, S45 0EW
T: 01246 590888
www.oldpoets.co.uk

Introduced by licensee Kim Beresford on his arrival at the pub in 2004, real cider and perry proved so popular, even though the Peak District isn't noted for its associations with cider, that within a couple of years the range had been built up from a single brand to six.

But then Kim is not one for doing things by halves. He also widened the choice of real ales at the Poet's to eight and started stocking Belgian beers both draught and bottled, and the next thing you know he'd got so carried away that he'd set up his own brewery in the cottage next door.

The draught cider and perry range at the Poet's extends to eight. Weston's Old Rosie is permanently on handpull, while down in the cellar – pity the barstaff's legs and order several pints at a time – are four ciders and three perries from different makers in polycask.

There's also a full menu including curry night every Sunday, a holiday cottage, and four B&B rooms. Oh, and Ashover claims to be the prettiest village not just in the county or in the Peak District, but in the whole country, having won the 2008 Calorgas award.

Runners up:

Banham Barrel

The Appleyard, Banham, Norfolk, NR16 2HE

T: 01953 888593

www.banhambarrel.co.uk

Penrhyn Arms

Pendre Road, Penrhynside, Conwy, Gwynedd, LL30 3BY

T: 07780678927

www.penrhynarms.com

Square & Compass

See p107

2005

Miners Arms

New Rd, Lydney, Gloucestershire, GL15 4PE

T: 01594 562483

www.minersarmswhitecroft.com

Named after the Forest of Dean's 'free miners' – forest dwellers who had the right to exploit the local coal-seams – this really is the country pub with everything. It has the River Lyd running past the front garden and a steam railway at the bottom of the child-friendly garden. There's a proper skittle alley as well as quoits and boules; a full menu served all day every day (except Tuesday); and five real ales on tap.

Oh, and up to 23 ciders. One of them is Strongbow, so we'll make that 22; but still! On handpump there are Thatcher's Traditional and Heritage and Mole's Black Rat; in bag-in-box are Weston's cloudy Old Rosie and Country perry; and the rest, in bottle, come from local makers including the Cadogan family from nearby Awre.

Runners up:

Brandy Wharf Cider Centre

Brandy Wharf, Waddingham, Lincolnshire, DN21 4RU

T: 01652 678364

Wellington

37 Bennetts Hill, Birmingham, B2 5SN

T: 0121 200 3115

www.thewellingtonrealale.co.uk

White Horse

Village Lane, Hedgerley, Buckinghammshire, SL2 3UY

T: 01753 643225

Dennis Gwatkin, owner of Gwatkin Cider, Herefordshire

Open Days, Museums and Visitor Centres

Cider, as I've said, is more than just a drink. It's a whole world of history and folklore, of toil and trouble, and, of course, of pleasure and leisure. And for all these reasons, it's an important plank in the structure of tourism in the main cidermaking regions. Visitors flock to farm tours to watch traditional milling and pressing techniques being demonstrated or simply to walk in the orchards. Museums large and small display ancient cidermaking and other farm equipment – and in most cases they have a licensed shop as well. There are open days and festivals, often with the added attractions of farmers' and craft markets and folk music and dance. In fact for many cidermakers the revenue tourism brings in is almost as important as the money they make from sales. So why not combine the two and try a cider holiday next year?

And if you do, here's a few attractions you might care to include on your itinerary.

Brogdale Horticultural Trust
Brogdale Farm, Brogdale Rd, Faversham, Kent, ME13 8XZ
T: 01795 535286
www.brogdale.org

Founded in 1952 on a 150-acre fruit farm to house the National Fruit Collections, Brogdale Horticultural Trust today has the world's largest collection of apple and pear varieties at 2,300 and 550 respectively. Its apples include a variety called Decio, which experts think might hark back as far as Roman times. And not only that, it has 350 varieties of plum, 320 of various soft fruits, and 220 of cherries. Oh, and nut-trees and grapevines as well.

Events throughout the year include Blossom Walks in March, Cherry and Strawberry Delights in July, a Summer Fruits Fiesta in August, a Cider

Left: old cider press and 'cheeses', Sheppys Cider, Tauton, Somerset

Barrels in the old tap room at Ross-on-Wye Cider and Perry, Herefordshire

Celebration in September, and an Apple Festival in October. There are also guided Orchard Walks year-round, and the Market Place has a range of shops including the Orchard Tearoom.

Gwynt y Ddraig open weekends
Llest Farm, Llantwit Fardre, Pontypridd, Glamorgan, CF38 2PW
T: 01443 217274
www.gwyntcider.com
Gwynt y Ddraig or Dragon's Breath is one of the great success stories of the craft cider revival. It was founded almost out of idle curiosity by Bill George and Drew Gronow in 2001, but after only their first batch they realised they were on to something and went commercial. In 2004 they became the first Welsh cidermaker to win CAMRA's Cider of the Year competition, and they've been winning awards at all sorts of events ever since.

In 2006 Gwynt y Ddraig won a listing with the national brewery of Wales, Brain's of Cardiff, thus becoming one of a tiny handful of craft cidermakers to be taken seriously by the brewing industry. And in August the same year the company held its first open weekend at Llest Farm, attracting several hundred local people over the two days to drink its cider, eat organic local burgers and other barbecue treats, and watch apples being milled and pressed. By 2008 the open weekends had become so popular that Gwynt y Ddraig held two, adding one in April.

Ross-on-Wye Cider Festival
Mike Johnson, Broome Farm, Peterstow, Ross-on-Wye, Herefordshire, HR9 6QG
T: 01989 567232
www.rosscider.com
The Festival was first held at the Yew Tree in Ross in 2003 and was sponsored by Broome Farm Cider.

Orchard walks at Ross-on-Wye Cider and Perry

In those days it was a one-day event with an outdoor bar selling a variety of ciders and perries from several local makers and a demonstration of milling and pressing, with live music throughout the day and a ceilidh in the evening.

By its third year the Festival had outgrown the pub and moved to Broome Farm itself; and in 2006 it was extended to a whole weekend, with an opening ceilidh on the Friday evening and a farmers' and craft market on the Sunday. In 2007 there were nine cidermakers from around the region in attendance on the Saturday, and the session proved so popular that for the 2008 Festival it had to be ticket-only.

The safety limit of 400 at a time, and the limited amount of camping space available, means you might not be able to get a ticket for the Festival itself. But don't worry: Broome Farm has plenty of events year-round including orchard walks, barbecues, morris dancing, blues and folk nights, and even classical recitals. The farm also does bed and breakfast and evening meals (at which non-residents are welcome); and its cider cellar is open year-round for the sale of cider and perry on draught, in bottle, and even in 10 or 20-litre wineboxes.

Ross-on-Wye Cider Festival is held on the last weekend in August or the first in September.

Hereford Cider Museum

21 Ryelands St, Hereford, HR4 0LW
T: 01432 354207, www.cidermuseum.co.uk

The grand-daddy of all cider museums public and private is, naturally enough, to be found in the capital of cider. And not just in the capital of cider, either, but in its (former) citadel: Percy Bulmer's original factory building in Ryelands Street.

The Museum moved in when Bulmer's moved out, and with support first from Bulmer's and more recently from Weston's soon became the intellectual heavyweight of the cider world. Not only does it boast the usual (although more copious than usual) collection of cidermaking artefacts, costrels, horn cups and other rusticana, it also displays more elevated articles such as 18th-century lead-crystal cider glasses and 19th-century watercolours of apples and pears, and has a research library of some repute. You are as likely to encounter PhD pomology students here as mere ciderlovers, in fact.

Old cider sign at Hereford Cider Museum

On top of all that, it's got a distillery. An old Norman still was moved in in 1984 and now makes not only cider brandy à la Calvados (although at a price that would make a Norman flinch), but pear brandy too.

Above and below: Hereford Cider Museum

A full programme of events throughout the year includes the Museum's own cider and perry competition in May, a prestigious event in these parts; and the Apple Day-related cidermaking festival in October is perhaps the biggest event of its kind in the country.

Somerset Rural Life Museum
**Abbey Farm, Chilkwell St, Glastonbury, BA6 8DB
T: 01458 831197
www.somerset.gov.uk/somerset/
culturecommunity/museums/somersetmuseums/
somersetrurallife/**

Every county, pretty much, has its museum of rural life, but not many of them can boast a setting quite as steeped in history as Somerset's. Not only is it in Glastonbury itself, folklore capital of Britain and a key site in Arthurian legend, but it's actually sited on a farm that includes the Abbey's 14th-century barn.

The centrepiece of the museum is a series of reconstructed Victorian rooms in the old farmhouse through which you can follow the life story of 19th-century farm labourer John Hodges (whose biography you can buy in the gift shop), from cradle to grave. But there is also a big collection of tools, implements and bygones pertaining to rural Somerset industries such as peat-digging, willow-growing, cheese making and of course, this being Somerset, cidermaking. Oh, and mud-horse fishing, a near-extinct way of fishing the tidal mudflats of the Severn estuary using a wooden sledge which both carries the fisherman's gear and stops him from sinking in the ooze.

Naturally, the museum has its own orchard (this is, after all, Avalon, the Celtic 'Isle of Apples') and beehives, as well as rare-breed sheep and poultry. There's a busy schedule of events and exhibitions year round, so if you're planning a visit ring ahead or check the website.

Cider at Home

Making *your own* Cider

If you like cider, why not have a go at making it? Turning apples each autumn into a delicious drink could get to be a habit, and you'd be involved in a satisfying craft to boot. So, when you're done with all the pies and tarts and frozen fruit laid down for the dark months ahead, turn what's left of your surplus apples into delicious cider and think of Christmas, or spring and summer evenings when you can go to the shed and take out a bottle of your own cool produce to savour and impress friends with. Remember, you made it, and what you've made is likely to be superior to much that you could buy. Your problem will be that the shed will get empty all too soon, which leads on to the first rule of cidermaking: always make enough!

Now that you're tempted, you'll be glad to know that you don't even need cider apples to make good cider. Some authorities will disagree, but there are many parts of Britain, especially in the east, where there is a long pedigree of good cidermaking which has never used cider apples. True, some of the best ciders are undoubtedly made using cider fruit, but most people will probably not have access to genuine cider apples, and shouldn't be put off by the fact. If you do have a supply of cider apples, all the better.

There is nothing mysterious about cider fruit. It is simply that over the years people have come to value its distinctive range of flavours for making the drink. Other apples were bred for their culinary or dessert value.

If you haven't got any apples, don't despair. A very cost effective way of getting your fruit is to pick your own from a local farm. You can find details of your nearest at www.pickyourown.info or www.pickyourown.org.

'Pick-Your-Own' grew rapidly in the 1970s with the widespread use of domestic freezers, but since then people have come to value the freshness of the produce on offer. It's an enjoyable experience just to be on the farm, to get what you want, and know the names of the apples you'll be eating or using for the cider. You'll also be supporting local food production and the environment.

Cooking apples are bred to be rich in acid, dessert apples for sweetness, and cider fruit to contain both of these elements along with varying amounts of mouth-puckering components called tannins, more commonly encountered in very strong brewed tea. In low concentration tannins play a big role in the overall richness, subtlety and nuances of flavour which characterises a good cider.

If you want to know the names of the apples in your garden – perhaps those you've used in your cidermaking – there are two organisations offering an identification service: Brogdale Horticultural Trust in Kent, home to the National Fruit Collection, and Marcher Apple Network (MAN). Send three well-formed specimens, preferably with a couple of leaves and a stalk, packed carefully in newspaper or bubble wrap to the respective organisations with the current fee payable. Although it is a difficult art, given the hundreds of different apples still in existence, Brogdale or MAN will identify your fruit for you within a month or so. Details of both organisations' addresses, the work they do and when they are identifying are available at www.brogdale.org and www.marcherapple.net.

You don't need sophisticated apparatus to make cider, but you do need a press and some basic equipment. Think of the press as a real investment for the future, to be brought into commission each autumn, then stowed away until the following year when once again apples appear on the radar. I could tell you of friends who started their illustrious cider careers using a kitchen mincer to get the juice out of their apples. What a labour! I could regale you with stories about others who used the spin cycle of their automatic washing machine ('Mind you, we cleaned out the detergent beforehand!'), putting the apple pulp in a pillowcase. What a work of ingenuity and sometimes desperation man is! But at the end of the day you will need a press. They come in many shapes and sizes to fit the scale of your ambitions. Simple single screw basket presses can be bought reasonably inexpensively or made (there are many good websites and books offering clear step-by-step instructions) or you could design your own using, for example, a hydraulic car jack. If you are thinking of a much greater production of cider, you'll need a much bigger press deploying layers of apple pulp contained in synthetic fibre cloths to build up a cheese. Your best bet might be to source any of these larger presses (often requiring renovation) at architectural salvage merchants or similar organisations. Or once again, you could build your own.

Prior to being put in the press, apples need to be converted into a finely divided, milled, or a soft pulpy state in order to extract the apple juice. Cider, after all, is simply fermented apple juice, though there are many different types and strengths that can be made. Traditionally, the apples would be milled or scratted by being put through toothed rollers, hand-turned or, later driven by steam engines or tractors. Nowadays, the best options are rather expensive all-stainless steel electric milling machines, though small hand-turned alternatives can be bought and are good for making, say, up to 20 or 30 gallons of juice in a day or so.

There are, however, two other ways of getting our apples into the sloppy, pulpy state we need without recourse to expensive equipment. The first approach is to get an approximately 3-4 inch diameter baulk of round timber, about 4½ feet tall, preferably hardwood (if you can't get this, square sectioned *untreated* softwood would also serve), and drill through, about 6 inches from the top, to take a piece of thick dowel which will function as a double handle. You also need a good quality sturdy plastic

'Manaccan Prinrose' apples

or stainless steel (not galvanised) bucket that will resist splitting. Quarter the apples, fill about a third of the bucket with these quartered pieces and bash them to a pulp, quitting when you've had enough and not attempting to make the last pip squeak! Primitive, you might say, but I think of it as low-tech, honourable labour and satisfying. You can even insert another piece of dowel lower down and have a double bash with a friend or child. Or you could just get the children to do the bashing (they love it!) while you have a good time sitting around supping ale or cider and chewing the fat with your friends.

A quieter alternative is simply to stuff your (temporarily rearranged) freezer full of your apples, freeze them for a day or two, then remove, thaw out and give the softened fruit a bit of a bash before putting it into the press.

Here is the basic equipment you'll need for your cidermaking, obtainable from any good home-brew shop:

- **Large plastic tub** or **clean plastic dustbin** in which to wash apples.
- **Sturdy split-proof**, preferably white, **bashing bucket and baulk of timber** OR **freezer space** OR **small manual scratting machine** (electric machine if you're flush).
- **Cider Press**. If using a small basket press, you'll also need a nylon straining bag, medium mesh, to go inside the basket (nylon net curtain is an acceptable alternative).
- **Clean 1-gallon glass fermentation demijohns** or **5-gallon plastic fermentation vessels** (they hold nearer 7 gallons up to the top).
- **Fermentation locks** – the 'bubbler' type are probably best.
- **Small tub/carton of good wine yeast** (eg *Saccharomyces banyanus*) **with yeast nutrients** (or buy these separately). Make sure you use within the use-by-date. Do not use home baking yeast.
- **2-metre length of clear, food-grade, plastic siphoning** (racking off) **tube**.
- **Small pack of sodium metabisulphite sterilising agent**.
- Sundry items such as **cotton wool, nylon long-handled bottle brush** etc.
- **Combined beer/wine hydrometer** for measuring potential alcoholic strength of your cider (optional).

Here is the step-by-step procedure for getting your apple juice and fermenting it to cider:

1 Cleanliness and sterilisation are important, but not worth making a huge fuss about. Make up a 'stock' solution of the sodium metabisulphite by dissolving 50g of solid in 500ml of cold water (i.e. a 10% solution) and keep this in a glass bottle with a plastic cork, labelled POISON and out of reach of children. Do the dissolving in a well-ventilated area to avoid inhaling any fumes.

2 Work with whatever apples are at your disposal, but if you haven't got cider fruit, then if possible mix up your pile of fruit to include a good percentage of sweet or sweetish dessert apples and similar proportion of cooking apples. You can add a small ration of crab apples to introduce tannin into the juice or experiment by adding either proprietary tannin or even a little very strong brewed tea. As a general precaution *do not* use windfall fruit from animal-grazed orchards (picked from the trees is fine). Discard mouldy fruit without compromise, though lightly bruised fruit is okay.

3 Three quarters fill your plastic tub with cold water and add 500ml of your sterilising solution. Wash your apples in the water, adding small quantities of fruit at a time, rubbing off dirt, soil, leaves, bloom etc. This should be done quickly and doesn't need to be done too obsessively.

4 Quarter the apples and bash, freeze, or otherwise mill as discussed.

5 Make up another batch of sterilising solution and pour this into your fermentation vessel. Now add approximatly 2 litres of cold water (so that you are effectively working with a 2% solution) and swill this round the vessel with its bung on, finally discarding the solution down sink or drain. If you are only making, say, one gallon of juice, then you can put the sterilising fluid back into your 'stock' bottle and re-use for another time. When you have sterilised each vessel *you must* wash out the residual sterilising fluid in the vessels with cold water a couple of times and discard this.

6 If using a small basket press, put milled apple (pomace) into the nylon bag and fill to about one half to two thirds full – not more – and extract the juice directly into your fermentation vessel. Remove the pressed apple cake (now called spent pomace) from the press to feed to chickens or pigs, or to use in your compost bin.

7 You are now ready to start fermenting. If you're curious to know what your final alcoholic strength of cider will be, now is the time to use your hydrometer. Otherwise, you may assume it will generally be somewhere between 3 and 7% abv, depending on the sweetness of your juice. (7% is strong for a naturally fermented cider).

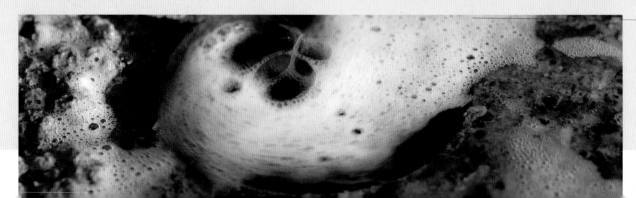

8 Add 1–2 heaped teaspoons of yeast per gallon of juice or, say, 3–4 per large fermentation vessel; the quantity isn't exactly critical (nine times out of ten you don't need to add any yeast, since the juice will ferment of its own accord, but what about the one time?) If bought separately, add the yeast nutrients now. Lightly plug vessel with cotton wool (*do not* fit fermentation lock yet); put vessel on a piece of newspaper and leave in a warmish place (a kitchen or utility room is ideal).

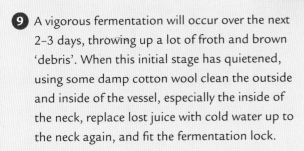

9 A vigorous fermentation will occur over the next 2–3 days, throwing up a lot of froth and brown 'debris'. When this initial stage has quietened, using some damp cotton wool clean the outside and inside of the vessel, especially the inside of the neck, replace lost juice with cold water up to the neck again, and fit the fermentation lock.

10 Depending on the sweetness of the juice and the ambient temperature, the fermentation will now proceed to dryness over a period anywhere between 3 weeks to 3 months. In a kitchen or warmish utility room this will probably take 4–5 weeks. Don't attempt to unduly speed up the fermentation by placing the barrel next to radiators or direct heat sources.

11 You'll know when to rack off (siphon off from the lees) by the fact that the young cider is now an almost clear golden colour and bubbles have stopped. You may notice the odd bubble coming up, but you do not need to wait for these to finish. On the other hand, do not attempt to bottle the young cider if it is at all cloudy, turbid, or anything other than very slightly hazy.

12 You can now do different things with your young cider. Either bottle it, say, in corked, sterilised wine bottles (filled to the top, thus excluding any air) OR store it in sterilised demi-johns – corked or bunged, or under fermentation lock. If you're not averse to using sugar, you may sweeten your demi-john of dry cider prior to drinking it but, a word of caution, use white sugar and sparingly. If you make the cider sickly, it will be undrinkable. You can start drinking this cider within a week or two, although it will 'round off' if left for a little longer.

13 Alternatively, you can turn your young racked cider into delicious bottled, naturally sparkling dry cider. This is my preferred cider. You need to work with slightly hazy young cider after siphoning off. If it isn't, add a very small amount of the lees back to the cider. What you are ultimately aiming for is the *merest* paint layer of these lees (mostly yeast) in each bottle. Use sterilised bottles that are designed to take pressure – 'clip top', 'crown' or plastic sealed screw top bottles. Measure carefully and add one level teaspoon of white sugar per pint, then siphon in the young racked cider, leaving a one inch gap at the head before putting on the top.

14 Store in a cool outhouse for at least 4–8 weeks over which period a delicious sparkle should develop. This should take you nicely up to Christmas & New Year, though don't forget to leave enough for those gorgeous summer evenings! Serve this particular type of cider very cold. Prost!

Cider and Food Matching

Interest in good food and in cookery is growing rapidly. A significant and growing number of people are now taking an interest in the quality of what they eat and drink, and also where and how it is produced.

Cider is something to be enjoyed with food, and a rising awareness of the different styles of cider and perry now available has served to increase the number of people that are enjoying matching cider with food. Like wine and beer, different styles and blends of cider lend themselves better to different types of food, and growing numbers of both cidermakers and chefs are developing ciders and menus that complement each other.

The discovery of the parallels between wine and cider is informing us about the possibilities. Cider and perry is made in the same way as wine is made – fermented from naturally extracted fruit juice. The juice of the different varieties of fruit (apples or perry pears in place of grapes) will produce different levels of sugar, acidity, tannin and astringency and it is the balance of these components that determine the taste profile of a drink. The differences in the juices from the different varieties of fruit used for cider and perry is as marked is it is with different grape varieties.

With over 400 cider apple varieties plus several hundred culinary and dessert apples to use, the cider maker has a seemingly limitless palate with which to blend. As a consequence, cidermakers are producing an ever-widening range of cider and perry, and this is accelerating the exploration of cider and food combinations. The innovation of single variety ciders are all part of this expanding repertoire, meaning cider makers are challenging the dominance of wine on the table.

Cider has the advantage that, at strengths ranging from 3% to 8.5% abv, it can be considerably less strong than wine, and about the same strength, if not rather stronger, than beer, allowing it to occupy a middle-ground on the dinner table, and for cider to replace both wine and beer as the dining public's accompaniment to a meal.

The fruit character and a taste profile that ranges from dry to sweet and from light to heavy make cider or perry a very versatile companion to different food groups. The natural acidity will also cut through the richest or spiciest of foods to refresh and offer contrast. As a rule, the less strong the cider or perry the sweeter it will be. An increasing number of products are now made by stopping the fermentation to leave a proportion of the sugars in the juice unchanged so encouraging a 'juicy' character rather than a 'vinous' character.

Perry is also enjoying a deserved revival as specialists are turning to this most subtle of fruit to make one of the rarest of our traditional alcoholic drinks. It is becoming increasingly available but still may take some searching out. As with cider, perry can be made from a single fruit variety or from a range of different blended juices, demonstrating the wide versatility of the drink.

Some pairings to consider:

Fish – the delicacy of fish is best complemented by a cider made from the lighter and fresher apples grown for eating or cooking. Or, for a fuller, richer but still subtle contrast, perry is an excellent match for fish. Several ciders are now made from mainly eating or dessert apples and it is well worth looking for a single variety cider for an individual taste. The options include ciders made from Cox, Katy or Spartan apples, and are now widely available in a range of strengths from 3.5% to 7.5% abv.

Pork – this can be a sweet and sometimes rather fat meat which, when roasted, is often served with apple sauce. Cider is therefore a natural accompaniment and has the versatility to suit both roast and grilled pork. It will also serve as a great match for a dish including pork, including casserole type dishes where cider might even be added to the pot.

With simply prepared pork, either a cider made exclusively from cider apple fruit or a single variety cider from a full-bodied cider apple, such as Somerset Redstreak or the famed Kingston Black variety, can bring a complexity of tannin balanced by acidity and sufficient sweetness. Other single varietal

ciders using the traditional bitter-sweet cider apples include Tremletts Bitter and Dabinett.

The creamy sauces often served with pork can be very rich and, again, cider can cut through to refresh and cleanse the palate. Here, the broad range of cider styles can work well and a decision can be made on the basis of whether a sweeter or a drier style is preferred – evidence of the versatility of cider.

Lamb – another sweet and possibly fat meat that is often prepared in similar manner to pork. For these reasons, the same choice of ciders is likely to serve although ciders made with a more robust cider apple such as Tremlett's Bitter may be preferred. A single varietal cider or one with a significant proportion of a cider apple like Tremlett's Bitter will have a high level of tannin and produce a cider of strong and robust character with a long finish.

Beef – conventional wisdom would pick cuts such as roast rib or steak for flavour, while the cheaper cuts deliver depth and richness in dishes from cottage pie to beef stew. The flavours of simply prepared beef may be accompanied by a lighter style of blended cider or a single variety cider, perhaps Dabinett or even a non-cider variety such as those suggested for fish. The fuller and richer flavours of stews or such dishes as cottage pie can be accompanied by most ciders but a drier, fuller style is probably best.

Cider is the most versatile of drinks. Not just great to quench a thirst, but also to match the food you plan to enjoy. Once you've experimented with a few combinations, you'll be able to select a cider or perry suited to your individual taste. Many people are also using cider and perry as a natural ingredient to include in a range of recipes. Cider and perry are fantastic ingredients to use in a wide range of dishes, but always remember to save some for the table!

Recipes

Real cider is a great accompaniment to all kinds of food, but also – like beer and wine – a fantastic ingredient to add flavour to your cooking. Apples and pork are a traditional combination, but cider can be used to create poultry, game and fish dishes too. Use it where you'd use wine in your cooking to add a fruity flavour, or deglaze a pan with it to make gravy.

Cider cuisine is taking off in pubs around the country, and a few of them have been kind enough to share their recipes. Try a few to whet your appetite and inspire you to seek out more, or even create your own.

Barbecued quails in real cider and five spices

Denise Thwaites, Maltsters Arms, Bow Creek, Tuckenhay, Devon, TQ9 7EQ

Serves 2

4 quails (ask your butcher to
   spatchcock them on skewers)
1–2 tbsps local honey
good pinch each of 5-spice
   powder, ginger, garlic and
   saffron
600ml (1 pint) real cider
sea salt and black pepper
2 aubergines and 3 different
   coloured peppers, thickly sliced

For the salsa:
1 large pepper
2 plumb tomatoes
1 red onion
2 cloves garlic
hot red chillies, to taste
1 tbsp caster sugar
white wine
tomato purée (optional)

For the sauce:
1 tbsp honey
1 tbsp butter

Spread some honey over each quail, skin side up, and sprinkle with 5-spice powder, saffron, ginger and garlic. Place in a deep dish, almost cover with cider, season and refrigerate overnight.

To make salsa, finely chop pepper, tomatoes, onion, garlic and chillies to taste. Add caster sugar and a generous slosh of white wine. Season to taste (add tomato purée to thicken if wished).

Barbecue the peppers and aubergines without oil until slightly blackened, then heat salsa in a pan and immerse peppers and aubergines in it for a few minutes. Barbecue the quails quite slowly to a golden brown colour – about 5 minutes each side.

To make sauce, pour a cupful of marinade into a pan, add a dollop each of honey and butter, and leave to bubble away until nice and gloopy.

Arrange peppers and aubergine on a plate, spoon salsa around, place 2 quails per portion on top and ladle over the sauce.

Scrumpy chicken pie

Elaine Foreman, Ring O'Bells, High Street, Ashcott, Bridgewater, Somerset, TA7 9PZ

Serves 2

1 large onion
3 sticks of celery
4 chicken legs
600ml (1 pint) scrumpy cider
1 chicken stock cube
100g natural yoghurt
175g grated Cheddar cheese
1 tbsp redcurrant jelly
cornflour, to thicken
500g potatoes, cooked and mashed
1 large carrot, grated
1 cooking apple, grated

Chop onion and celery and sweat off in a little oil. Add the chicken legs to the pan with the celery and cook – until lightly brown – to seal them.

Add the cider, bring to the boil and cook until the chicken legs are tender.

Remove chicken legs and put to one side to cool. Meanwhile reduce the cider by boiling fast until you have about half the quantity. Now add the stock cube and mix until it dissolves. Add the yoghurt, cheese and redcurrant jelly, and thicken sauce with the cornflour.

When chicken is cold, remove meat from the bones, dice and put it into the sauce. Pour the mixture into a dish.

Grate the carrot and apple into the mashed potato, mix well and spread over the chicken mixture. Brush the top with melted butter, or sprinkle with a little more grated cheese.

Bake in moderate oven (180°C/350°F/Gas mark 4) for about 45 mins.

Somerset pork chops

Elaine Foreman, Ring O'Bells, High Street, Ashcott, Bridgewater, Somerset, TA7 9PZ

Serves 2

2 pork chops
2 tbsp Cheddar cheese, grated
2 tbsp Bramley apple, grated
150ml Somerset cider
150ml double cream
salt and pepper

With a sharp knife make a horizontal cut into each chop to make a pocket. Stuff the grated cheese and apple into the pocket and secure the two edges together with a cocktail stick.

Grill the chops until cooked.

When the chops are cooked, put in a saucepan with a wide base and add the cider. Put on maximum heat to boil the cider and reduce it by half.

Then add the cream and continue to boil rapidly until the sauce is thick. Adjust the seasoning and serve immediately.

Rabbit braised with cider

Simon Imrie, Pembury Tavern, 90 Amhurst Road, Hackney, E8 1JH

If you're lucky enough to live near a source of local wild rabbits, this can be a cheap and easy dish. Wild rabbits are not so easy to come by in Hackney, however, and I often buy farmed rabbits from my butcher. They are larger and meatier that their wild cousins, and will feed more mouths. I serve this dish with whatever seasonal vegetables are around; it goes well with some minted new potatoes.

Serves 2–3

1 rabbit, cut into 6 pieces
300ml (½ pint) cider
300ml (½ pint) chicken stock
sprig of rosemary
sprig of thyme
2 bay leaves
salt & pepper to taste

Preheat the oven to gas 180°C/350°F/Gas mark 4

Place the ingredients in a casserole dish, preferably one with a snuggly fitting lid, but tightly wrapping in kitchen foil also works. The idea is to keep as much steam in as possible. If you are using instant stock, it's a bad idea to add salt at this stage, as by the time the dish is cooked the saltiness can become too intense.

Cook the rabbit for 1½ to 2 hours, depending on the size of rabbit, or until tender.

Take the rabbit pieces, thyme, bay and rosemary out of the liquid, and pour the liquid into a saucepan. Boil the sauce until half of it has evaporated. Season if necessary.

Serve the rabbit with some seasonal vegetables and pour the sauce over. Pour a glass of cider to drink with the meal.

Pork with cider & cream

Michael Pooley, *Real Cidermaking on a Small Scale*

As variants to this, try substituting the pork with chicken breasts or legs, or rabbit joints. The onion can be replaced with several cloves of garlic which should be lightly fried until soft and translucent, then removed, to be added and mashed in once the cider sauce has been made.

Serves 4

250ml dry cider
4 pork chops or steaks
1 medium-sized onion
50g mushrooms
2 tbsp plain flour
salt and pepper
60g butter
150 ml single cream
1 tbsp chopped parsley
1 tbsp chopped chives

Chop the onion finely. In a deep frying pan, melt the butter and fry the onion until golden. Season the flour and use half to coat the pork. Fry the chops or steaks lightly until brown on each side and then remove.

Chop the mushrooms and fry lightly, mixing in with the onion. Turn down to a very low heat, stir in the remaining seasoned flour to make a basic roux with the butter and then gradually add the cider, stirring all the while. Bring to the boil for a minute. Season with a little salt and pepper, return the pork to the pan, cover and simmer on a low heat for 20 minutes or until the pork is tender.

Now stir in the cream and the chopped herbs. Serve with boiled new potatoes and runner or French beans.

Fish in cider

Michael Pooley, *Real Cidermaking on a Small Scale*

Serves 4

250ml dry cider
4 white fish steaks or fillets
30g butter
salt and pepper
juice of half a lemon
1 beef tomato
60g mushrooms
30g plain flour
1 tbsp chopped parsley

Put the fish in a greased baking dish and top with sliced tomatoes and mushrooms. Season with salt and pepper, add the lemon juice and pour in the cider. Cover the dish with a lid or foil and bake in a moderately hot oven (200°C/400°F/Gas mark 6) for about 20-25 minutes.

Drain the liquid off from the fish, keeping it to one side. Melt the butter in a heavy saucepan, stir in the flour to make a basic roux and now slowly add in the reserved liquid to make the sauce, stirring all the while and bringing to the boil for 1 minute.

Pour the sauce over the fish and garnish with chopped parsley. Serve with mashed or boiled potatoes and seasonal vegetables.

Somerset cider and honey syllabub

Elaine Foreman, Ring O'Bells, High Street, Ashcott, Bridgewater, Somerset, TA7 9PZ

This recipe is best made the day before you want to serve it as the flavour will improve overnight.

Serves 2

275ml double cream
125ml Somerset cider
75g honey
caster sugar, to taste

Place cream, cider and honey in bowl and whip until thick. Check sweetness and add more honey or caster sugar to your taste, (and depending on sweetness of the cider you are using).

Place into wine glasses and refrigerate.

Summer cider punch

Michael Pooley, *Real Cidermaking on a Small Scale*

As variants to this, replace the lemon peel with any or all of the following: pieces of orange, cucumber, mint.

Serves 8

1 litre real cider
1 litre lemonade or soda water
rind of 1 lemon
juice of half a lemon
25 ml whisky
25 ml gin
caster sugar

Chill the cider and lemonade and mix in a large bowl or jug.

Cut up the lemon rind and add, along with the other ingredients, sweetening to taste.

Mulled cider

Michael Pooley, *Real Cidermaking on a Small Scale*

Serves 4

1 litre fresh cider
12 whole cloves
1 stick of cinnamon
12 white/green cardamom seeds
pinch of grated nutmeg
caster sugar

Choose a suitable mulling vessel – avoid aluminium or non-stick, but a glass or ordinary stainless steel pan is suitable. A stainless steel 'maslin pan' of 2–3 litre capacity is ideal.

Gently simmer the cider with the spices for 20 minutes or so.

Dissolve a little white sugar into the mulled cider according to preferred taste and serve hot in a tumbler or wine glass.

For a drink with a slightly bigger 'kick', add a measure of light or dark rum to each glass beforehand.

Hot cider toddy

Michael Pooley, *Real Cidermaking on a Small Scale*

Serves 1

250ml real cider
2 cloves
root ginger
1 tsp lemon juice
1 tbs honey

Roughly chop the root ginger. Add the cider, cloves and lemon juice, and simmer for a minute in a stainless steel or enameled pan.

Strain off into a glass and add the honey to taste.

Where to buy Cider

While it is relatively easy to enjoy real cider and perry at the pub, at a cider house, at a CAMRA beer and cider festival or purchased direct from the producer – what should you do if you want to drink it at home with Sunday lunch or give it to a friend as a present? In truth this is a difficult and complicated area which this section hopes to guide you through to allow you to make informed choices.

You may think I am being overly melodramatic by highlighting the difficulties associated with drinking real cider and perry at home – but the key consideration here is 'Is it Real?' The bottled ciders and perries widely available in your local off licence or not-quite-so-supermarket will probably be pasteurised, carbonated and possibly micro filtered which means they are no longer 'real' products. Their yeast has been killed off by pasteurization, extraneous gas has been forced into the product at a molecular level by carbonation, and the micro filtering will have stripped away layers of flavour – leaving a consistent product, which lacks the timeless artesian techniques you may imagine you have been buying into. A small number of producers do not pasteurise their products when bottling – however it is best to ask them individually about this as techniques can alter.

If you want to enjoy real cider and perry at home, it might be best to arrange to visit a producer regularly, talk to your local pub which sells real products and see if you can purchase some from them, visit CAMRA festivals and purchase a take away container from the cider and perry bar, or visit a specialist shop. Like wine it's best to purchase what you like – but that where the similarity ends. Unlike wine, cider and perry are not bought to be laid down and it then drunk once they have matured: cider and perry are ready for consumption as soon as the producer judges them ready and puts them on sale. The products can vary in colour through the spectrum from gold to amber to brown and can be clear or hazy, depending on the techniques and processes used by the producer – the one thing to look out for is lumps as this may indicate the product has not settled or that things are not quite as they should be.

So how can you expect to purchase real cider or perry? Usually it is dispensed from a larger container into a new two or four pint plastic carton similar to the kind used for milk. This carton should be squeezed slightly as it's filled to allow the cider or perry to reach the brim and the top put firmly in place to ensure that as little air as possible remains within the carton. One notable producer used to use a length of rubber hosing which reached into the bottom of the container thereby minimizing the splashing action of the cider or perry filling the carton and reducing the contact and subsequent reaction between the air and the product. Air is the biggest threat to real cider and perry as it will rapidly oxidise and go bad, so anything you can do to ensure you reduce air contact, the longer your product will last. I am reliably told of the tapping of an undiscovered 50-year-old barrel. While the

Storing cider at Hecks Farmhouse Cider, Somerset

cider inside was the usual yellow colour when poured, it turned black within two or three minutes as it reacted with the oxygen – and while it was still relatively drinkable, it had lost its depth of flavour. Cider does not age in the same way as wine – although you can find several vintage varieties for sale, which are between three and five years old and have mellowed well.

Producers tend to supply their products to licensed premised in polycasks. These are like mini plastic casks and are usually brown or black in colour with an airlock or vent in the top which allows the product to breath, and they hold 40 pints or five gallons. Real cider or perry in one of these polycasks can last seven to ten days (as long as the vent at the top is closed when not in use) and they make an interesting addition and talking point to the top of many a bar counter. These must be arguable the most flexible and easily recyclable dispense method as once empty they are returned washed out and used again, thereby creating a sustainable supply system.

Sometime you may come across bag-in-a-box systems – the key here is whether they have been cold filled or filled at temperature. If they are cold filled the bag is just a smaller version of the polycask and the product is real and has a similar life span. However if they are hot filled it is possible that the yeast has been killed off and therefore the product inside is no longer real. Should you be presented by the bag in the box system it is worth asking which method was used and making your own decision as to whether this is the type of product for you.

Despite what is suggested by the French, the use of *Methodé Champenoise* and mushroom corks were not pioneered in France – it was developed in Somerset. Nationally we produce some excellent *Methodé Champenoise* ciders and perries and I would highlight Burrow Hill, Ashridge, Gospel Green, Yarde, and Butford as all being superb.

Outlets

National Collection of Cider & Perry
Middle Farm, Firle, Lewes, East Sussex, BN8 6LJ
01323 811324
www.middlefarm.com

The National Collection of Cider & Perry is a unique celebration of our national fruit. Visitors can taste, compare and buy from a range of over 100 different draught ciders and perries (including Middle Farm's own Pookhill Cider).

As well as a huge range of meads, country wines and fruit liqueurs, the Collection holds a carefully selected range of draught and bottled ales. They also stock English cider brandy and eau de vie. Fresh apple juice is pressed daily, and an apple-pressing service is offered throughout the late summer and autumn.

In addition there is a working farm and farm shop with over 20 types of sausage and 50 types of cheese and lots of delightful gifts and presents to appeal to every age group. Truly a destination location.

Please be aware when purchasing bottles that not all contain real products!

Orchard Hive & Vine
01568 613576
www.orchard-hive-and-vine.co.uk

Orchard Hive & Vine are an online cider, wine and beer stockist in Leominster, Herefordshire – just 12 miles or so from the Welsh border. They specialise in the supply of quality produce, delicious cider and perry, mead, special beers and ales, apple juice, English and Welsh wine, as well as many other wines and liqueurs from elsewhere. The products are available for home delivery through their online catalogue. They also stock a refreshing, inclusive and interesting selection of ciders and perries local to the Leominster area – meaning that it's always well worth checking out what is available.

Green Valley Complex
Darts Farm Village, Topsham, Exeter, Devon, EX3 0QH
01392 878200
www.dartsfarm.co.uk

Not only can you purchase Green Valley products but also a range of other ciders and perries. There is a wide range of toys and food in this innovatively diverse selection that will make any foodie stop in their tracks and be thankful that they visited.

York Beer and Wine shop
28 Sandringham Street, Fishergate, York, YO10 4BA
01904 647136
www.yorkbeerandwineshop.co.uk

A varied and interesting selection where the majority of ciders come from the small band of cider makers, dedicated to making the natural product using only whole cider fruit with no additives. Consequently the range fluctuates depending on availabilty (apples are, after all, a seasonal fruit) but normally includes ciders (and perries) from Dunkertons, Burrow Hill, Minchews and Sheppy's. Draught cider from Thatchers is also available, supplemented by 'guest' ciders from many other producers, as supplies permit. These include Wilkins, Naishs, Summers, Hartlands and Lyne Down, to name but a few.

Markets

Many smaller cider and perry producers participate in their local farmers' market. You can check where farmers market are being held via: www.farmersmarket.net

Five of the best markets to visit are:

Borough Market

Southwark Street, London, SE1 1TL
www.boroughmarket.org.uk
On Thursdays, Fridays and Saturdays, the place to be in London is the award-winning Borough Market where Barry Topp has his New Forest Cider outlet and hosts numerous other producers' products. Truly a delight.

Bristol's Slow Food Market

Corn Street, Bristol, BS1 1HT
www.slowfoodbristol.org
Founded in 2004, Bristol's Slow Food Market was the first Slow Food market in the world to be regularly held, and is now the largest food market in Bristol. The quality and range of produce offered for sale at the market all conform to the principles of Slow Food, which supports traditional, regional and seasonal foods. Oliver's Cider and Perry, and French cider importers Quality French Ciders have stalls.

Greenwich Covered Market

Greenwich Church Street, London, SE10 9HZ
www.greenwich-market.co.uk
The Orchard Press Cider Company operates out of the Food Court in Greenwich Covered Market, south London. Currently their specialist range is sourced from a variety of small producers across 40 square miles of beautiful open countryside, orchards & farms deep inside Normandy, France and also from producers in West Sussex.

Stroud Farmers' Market

Cornhill Market Place, Stroud, Gloucestershire
www.fresh-n-local.co.uk/markets/stroud.php
The National Farmers' Retail & Markets Association Farmers' Market of the Year 2008 is well-known as one of the busiest and most popular farmers market in the UK. It is held every Saturday and features 45 producers, including up to 10 organic producers. An outlet for Lyne Down Cider.

Teme Valley Market

The Talbot, Knightwick, Worcester, WR6 5PH
01886 821235
www.the-talbot.co.uk/teme_valley_market.htm
The Teme Valley Market has been trading since October 1998 making it one of the oldest farmers markets in the country. It is held at the Talbot at Knightwick, in the heart of the Three Counties countryside on the second Sunday of the month, and is an outlet for Olivers Ciders and Perry as well as Mill Orchards, Frome Valley Vineyard and the Teme Valley Brewery.

National Cider and Perry Championships

CAMRA's annual cider and perry competition is held in May, and hosted by the Reading Beer and Cider Festival with two days of keenly-awaited judging.

2008

Gold Cider Winner – Green Valley Farmhouse Vintage Cyder (Exeter, Devon)
"A lovely 'proper cider' aroma, like an Autumn morning. It was easy drinking with a pleasant lingering aftertaste."

Silver Cider Winner – West Croft Janet's Jungle Juice (Highbridge, Somerset)
Bronze Cider Winner – Blaengawney Cider (Newport, Gwent)

Gold Perry Winner – Gregg's Pit Perry (Much Marcle, Herefordshire)
"A balance of citrus aroma with a winey aftertaste. Fabulous."

Silver Perry Winner – Ross-on-Wye Cider and Perry (Ross-on-Wye, Herefordshire)
Bronze Perry Winner – Hartland's Perry (Tirley, Gloucestershire)

2007

Gold Cider Winner – West Croft Janet's Jungle Juice (Highbridge, Somerset)
Silver Cider Winner – Cornish Orchards Dry (Liskeard, Cornwall)
Bronze Cider Winner – Green Valley Cyder Vintage Farmhouse (Exeter, Devon)

Gold Perry Winner – Hartlands (Tirley, Gloucestershire)
Silver Perry Winner – Newton Court (Newton, Leominster, Herefordshire)
Bronze Perry Winner – Gwatkin Malvern Hills (Abbey Dore, Herefordshire)
Highly Commended – Minchews (Tewkesbury, Gloucestershire)

2006

Gold Cider Winner – Hecks Kingston Black (Street, Somerset)
"Ripe fruity aroma… This cider lingers on the tongue and makes it burst into flower."

Silver Cider Winner – Harechurch Dry (Drybrook, Gloucestershire)
Bronze Cider Winner – Dening's Medium (Near Yeovil, Somerset)
Bottled Cider Winner – Steve Hughes (Llandegla, Wrexham, North Wales)

Gold Perry Winner – Seidr Dai (Cardiff)
Silver Perry Winner – Ross-on-Wye (Broom Farm) (Peterstow, Hereford)
Bronze Perry Winner – Mr Whiteheads (Newton Valence, Hampshire)

2005

Gold Cider Winner – Ralph's 3B's Cider (New Radnor, Powys)
Silver Cider Winner – Upton Sweet (Didcot, Oxfordshire)
Bronze Cider Winner – Newton Court Medium (Herefordshire)

Gold Perry Winner – Gwynt Y Ddraig (Llantwit Fardre, Glamorgan)
"Mellow with slight honey notes, with an aroma of fruit and toffee and a clean dry finish."

Silver Perry Winner – Minchew's (Tewkesbury, Gloucestershire)
Bronze Perry Winner – Hecks Farmhouse (Street, Somerset)

2004

Gold Cider Winner – Gwynt Y Ddraig Medium (Llantwit Fardre, Glamorgan)
Silver Cider Winner – Upton Sweet (Didcot, Oxfordshire)
Bronze Cider Winner – Dunkertons Medium (Pembridge, Herefordshire)

Gold Perry Winner – Gwatkin Blakeney Red (Abbey Dore, Herefordshire)
Silver Perry Winner – Summers (Berkley, Gloucestershire)
Bronze Perry Winner – Butford Farm Dry (Bodenham, Herefordshire)

Cider
Abroad

Introduction

There's a horizontal strip across Europe where everything is just perfect – the so-called 'Cider Belt'. Go any further south and it's far too hot, so the locals have to resort to making wine. Go any further north and it's too cold, so beer is reluctantly the order of the day. Those poor souls up in places like Russia and Scotland, have to make do with spirits.

Colonising Europeans took apple trees to the New World where pioneer nurseryman Johnny Appleseed became part of American folklore for his orchard-planting, and apples and cider entered American culture. Prohibition put paid to cider-culture in the 1920s, but a few US cidermakers are starting to produce real 'hard' (fermented) ciders again, and across the border in Quebec, cidermakers are learning from German ice wines to make award-winning and uniquely Canadian ice ciders.

The temperate climate of Europe's Cider Belt gives rise to a landscape and a culture that's all pastures and orchards, all cheeses and cider. At the eastern end we have Austria, Germany and southern Scandinavia, with their perry and ciders respectively. The Hardanger region of Norway flies the flag for Scandinavian craft cider, with production of cider from wild apples dating back to the late 18th century. Prohibition knocked cider culture here as well, but several producers have reinvested in cider culture and are now selling to the licensed trade.

In the central section we have northern France, and over the channel our own bit of cider paradise in South-West England and South-East Wales, as well as Jersey in between, which is working to preserve a longstanding cider heritage that includes many unique varieties of cider apple. The western section, however, is where cidermaking started; where specialist equipment was first used to mill and press selected varieties of cider apple as far back as the 11th century – northern Spain.

Imported real ciders are much harder to get hold of in the UK than the home-grown stuff – barring one or two specialist retailers and restaurants – so the best way to taste foreign ciders and perries and see cider culture abroad is to seek it out at its source.

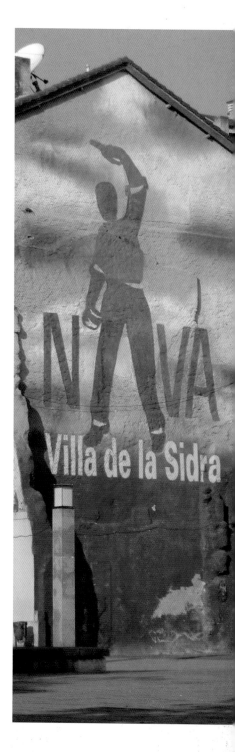

Europe's Cider Regions

SWEDEN

North Sea

DENMARK

Baltic Sea

Copehagen

Edinburgh

Belfast

Hamburg

Berlin

Dublin

IRELAND

UNITED KINGDOM

NETHERLANDS

Amsterdam

The Hague

GERMANY

London

Brussels

BELGIUM

Frankfurt am Main

Prague

CZECH REPUBLIC

LUXEMBOURG

Luxembourg

The Viezstrasse

Vienna

ATLANTIC

Pays d'Auge

Paris

Cornouaille

Domfront

Mostviertel

AUSTRIA

OCEAN

SWITZERLAND

LIECHTEN STEIN

SLOVAKIA

Bern

Ljubljana

FRANCE

ALPS

Lyon

Milan

Bay of Biscay

Turin

Bordeaux

ITALY

Asturias

Bilboa

Marseille

Pyrenees

ANDORRA

Corsica

Rome

The Basque Country

Barcelona

Naples

Sardinia

PORTUGAL

Madrid

SPAIN

Balearic Islands

Lisbon

Mediterranean Sea

Sevilla

N

0   100   200km

Spain

Of the four regions of Spain strung across the northern Atlantic shoreline, two have a strong and ancient cider tradition – Asturias in the west and the Basque Country to the east. Both regions have many things cider-related in common, but each has a cider culture that is unique and individual, and that makes each well worth a separate visit.

Natural cider in Spain is labelled '*Sidra Natural*' and is unfiltered and invariably a little cloudy. Look for this phrase on bottles and in bars if you want to try the full-flavoured, pure-juice, natural ciders of Spain, and avoid the more industrial, processed versions. Asturias has secured the European PDO (Protected Designation of Origin) mark, signifying its ciders' quality and origin, so any bottles carrying '*DOP Sidra de Asturias*' are particularly recommended.

Asturias

Asturias is an unspoilt, picturesque region with mountains, coastline, and the strongest cider culture of anywhere in the world. Around 70 cider companies make an annual 45 million litres of natural cider, and it's drunk by everyone in specialist cider bars called *sidrerias*.

Villaviciosa

Villaviciosa is the 'Apple Town' of Spain. It's only a small place, but it's got about 20 *sidrerias* all selling pure-juice, unpasteurised, un-carbonated and unfiltered *sidra*. I managed to visit about ten. In each the barman opens a bottle of cider, pouring a shot by holding the bottle above his head and the glass by his waist. The thin glass resonates generating thousands of tiny swirling bubbles, and the cider then has to be drunk before the foam subsides. Lovely!

Natural cider pouring in Sidreria Ballera, Villaviciosa

Spanish cider is similar to ours, but perhaps a little less tannic, and a little more sharp. Sidreria El Cañu is a good starting point. Like every other *sidreria* in town it has a tiled floor, wooden tables and chairs, hanging hams, and a television which is always on but no-one ever watches. Unlike most other *sidrerias* it also has an old cider press on display, and carefully preserved collections of cider bottles and cider glasses. Bright, colourful and friendly, it's a real advert for Asturian cider.

In a couple of places I order a selection of tapas – cured ham, local cheeses, that kind of thing. Seafood is popular, and the local speciality, in season, is sea urchins, which you have to cut in half before scooping out the insides with a teaspoon.

Cangas de Onis

From Villaviciosa, it's a short drive down to the quaint fishing village of Tazones for coffee and a paddle in the sea, or a longer drive to Cangas de Onis – via a stunning viewpoint in the hills – for a late lunch. Cangas de Onis was the first capital of modern Spain at the start of the fight-back against the Moorish invaders. Cangas's ten or so *sidrerias* include the impressive El Polesu. Most memorable, however, is La Sifoneria, a friendly little place with tiled walls, cider from Trabanco, and a huge collection of soda siphons.

In the summer Cangas can draw in a good few Spanish tourists, due in part to its close proximity to Covadonga. This was the site of the first battle victory the Spanish Christians recorded against the occupying Moors, and today has a monastery and cave housing a chapel that are worth a visit en-route to the *Picos de Europa* (Peaks of Europe) National Park. At the right time of year you can find snow at the top of the mountains, and the view over the lakes is made even more beautiful by the clear blue sky and the vultures circling over the valley below.

Trabanco glasses and bottle

Nava

Nava is the 'Cider Town of Spain', and hosts an annual cider festival in July. See the town council website, www.ayto-nava.es for details.

In Nava I met up with old friend Osoro. He's employed by the local cidermakers as President of their association, and one of his duties is to greet and look after visiting cidermakers. There are around 70 commercial cidermakers in Asturias, each making anything between tens of thousands and four million litres of natural cider. Osoro took me to visit one in Nava itself. Sidra Viuda de Corsino is right in the centre of town, next door to the excellent Sidreria La Figar. Their cider is stored in huge vats – either stainless steel conicals or, more romantically, great barrels of chestnut – each holding in the region of 20,000 litres. And they're not stingy about giving us some samples either. Each of the great vats has a tiny tap, which our host opens, releasing a thin jet of cider horizontally, to be caught expertly in a glass held at arm's length. The cider is fresh, appley and lovely. There are lots of vats and we try nearly all of them, just to be polite you understand.

What's that Osoro? Another cidermaker to visit? If you insist! And so we trot off to see Sidra Roza run by the inscrutable and hospitable Juan Roza.

None of your stainless steel with Juan, all of his cider is in chestnut, and lovely it was too, balanced

Juan Roza pouring from his barrels made of chestnut

and moreish, fresh and fruity. This was my third visit to Roza, but the first time I had ever been invited to see the 'Sistine Chapel of Cider', as Osoro proudly introduced it. In an adjoining building, old and rustic with stone walls and tiled roof, we marvelled at two rows of huge and ancient chestnut barrels. Beautiful and timeless – the whole place can't have changed in hundreds of years.

Sidreria Barraca is one of the many popular *sidrerias* of Nava, and home to Suzanna Ovin, former Asturian Cider Pouring Champion. As always she pours with unerring accuracy, the golden stream of cider falling directly between her eyes. Each shot or *culin* is exactly one sixth of a bottle. On a busy Friday or Saturday night she'll be pouring almost non-stop – hard work but well worth the effort. In effect, you can only have a drink when the pourer has a moment to serve you, and this takes a bit of getting used to. But once familiar with it, it becomes part of the attraction.

Oviedo

Osoro also lined up a visit to a modern orchard, where the owner had built a house with an observation tower, from which we were able to look over his hectares of trees and across to the plains beyond. I was staggered to discover that cider apples fetch 50c per kilo, which equates to €500 per tonne, or about £400. Compare that to eighty quid per tonne we get back home! Our host isn't a commercial cidermaker, but made several thousand litres as a bit of a 'hobby' – again it is gorgeous, and perhaps the most British tasting of the Asturian ciders I've tried.

Trabanco is Asturias's largest cidermaker, producing an annual four million litres of natural, pure-juice cider in the hills beside the city of Gijon. Trabanco's Marketing Manager José Mañuel is our genial host, and gives us a tour of the facility. 'We've got 13 huge traditional wooden presses,' he tells us in front of four of them, 'each of which takes between eight and 13 tonnes of apple pulp at once. The pulp is first macerated in steel conicals, and after pressing the juice is stored in 31,000 litre fibreglass settling tanks. All fermentation happens in the huge chestnut barrels using natural yeasts and no sulphite. The finished cider is blended', José Mañuel explains, 'to give it the cidermaker's personality.' He gave us some samples from one of his towering chestnut *tonles* (barrels) and it was predictably delicious, foaming white against the gold liquid, cool and refreshing, fruity and sharp, with a long satisfying finish.

At Trabanco, we are treated to a five-course meal in their *sidreria* which has a view to die for. Ham croquettes are followed by mussels in a cider sauce. Then comes salt cod with fried onions, followed by outstanding steak on the bone garnished with crystals of sea salt. Those with room left have a couple of traditional puddings. The whole lot is washed down with copious amounts of Sidra Trabanco, and we were introduced to Trabanco's impressive new champagne-style cider called Poma Áurea, presented in a unique and stylish bottle. Dragging ourselves away from the *sidreria* it was off for one last treat, one I'd heard about but never seen. Trabanco have bought a disused railway tunnel that curves its way into the

Samuel Trabanco viewing a sample

rock of the hillside. In it they store cider – in 38 cylinders each containing 22,000 litres. A stunning sight never to be forgotten.

Time for a rant. Why can't the larger UK cidermakers make a pure-juice, natural product? Why all the watering, the filtering, the pasteurisation? Trabanco is living proof that you can make great cider on a huge scale. Why not us Brits? Part of the answer is consistency. In Asturias, the customer accepts that each barrel is different, it's part of the cider culture there. In the UK, the customer demands that each pint is exactly the same as the previous one. I think that it's time to re-educate the British public!

Oviedo is a university city, and Real Oviedo FC were the last stop on Stan Collymore's professional career. Osoro was on hand with an impromptu walking tour of the historic and fascinating old part of the city. Oviedo has dozens of *sidrerias*. Conveniently, six or more are situated on the same street – Calle Gascona – which a hanging neon sign at either end proudly proclaims to be 'El Bulevar de la Sidra'. Over the evening I quiz Osoro on what makes a good *sidreria*. There are four main things, according to our resident expert:

- cider stored at the correct temperature
- good cider pourers
- the right number of customers, not too many or too few
- some tradition and history – a good sidreria might be passed down through the same family for generations

Basque Country

The recorded history of cidermaking in the Basque Country dates from as far back as April 1014. Legend has it that northern Spain is where cidermaking all began, initially using apple trees growing wild around the farms. From here, so the theory goes, cidermaking spread north and east into France and England. Today about 75 cidermakers in the Basque Country produce roughly nine million litres a year of natural cider, called *sagardo* in the Basque tongue, and they are centered around the village of Astigarraga, just a few kilometres inland from San Sebastian ('Donostia' in Basque). Unlike the Asturian tradition of specialist cider bars, the Basques normally drink their cider at the cider farms or *sagardotegias*. It's a great evening out, and all Basques will visit *sagardotegias* for birthdays, anniversaries, and other social occasions. As well as cider, there's a set menu of rustic food, and a great tradition of accordion playing with spontaneous singing and improvised poetry recitals.

Astigarraga

Sagardotegia Gartziategi is a typical Basque cider farm, modest-looking on the outside, much more impressive in. Two connected rooms have a wooden beamed roof, held up with wooden pillars. The walls are rough stone, and on the concrete floor are some long wooden tables, but no chairs. What really catches the eye is the row of eleven huge barrels, each taller than a man, each holding several thousand litres of cider. One barrel has a small brass tap from which you are allowed to help yourself. Opening the tap with one hand, a thin stream of cider jets out and has to be caught in the glass in your other outstretched hand, some two metres away! Drunk down before the bubbles subside it's gorgeous – dark yellow and aromatic, appley and light with a lemony sharpness. We stand at the tables for the first course, melt-in-the-mouth cod omelette. Then a cry of '*Txotx!*' (pronounced a bit like 'church') from Bitor Lizeaga, the proprietor. This means that one of the other ten barrels is on offer, and Bitor fits a key into the tap, turning it on. One by one we file up to the barrel with our glasses, catching a shot of streaming gold liquid, one glass moving up towards the barrel behind the other so as not to spill a drop.

Inside of Sagardotegia Gartziategi

Outside of Sagardotegia Gartziategi

This cider is a little less sharp, perhaps a little more tannic, but just as good.

And so the meal continues; different courses of food arrive, punctuated by frequent cries of '*Txotx!*'. Fried cod with onions is next, followed by steak on the bone, again covered in big crystals of salt. To finish, Idiazabal sheep cheese with quince jelly, then small, dark tasty walnuts and spring-loaded nut crackers. Each barrel of cider is subtly different, but all complemented the food perfectly. The reason for the lack of chairs quickly becomes apparent. What with all the coming and going to the barrels, you keep changing places, and so meet all kinds of people. Local girl Aurkene confided that Bitor has 'a neat Basque accent', and a bunch of French Basques who had come over the border by bus become my new best friends. At one point Bitor cries '*Txotx*' and walks out of the front door! We all follow him to a neighbouring building to sample another two barrels, and where I finally get the chance to have a chat with him. 'I make about 100,000 litres of cider per year,' he tells me, 'using about 50 varieties of apples, half of which will be sharps, 40% sweets, and 10% bitter varieties. Usually, only half of our apples are local, so we have to import apples from Asturias, Galicia or even Normandy.'

San Sebastian

The *sagardotegia* cider season only lasts from January to April, so for the rest of the year Basque cider fans must rely upon bottled natural cider in the bars and restaurants. One of the best places for a bar crawl is the old quarter in San Sebastian, a square mile of streets laid out in a medieval grid pattern. You could easily lose a day or two wandering from one to the other trying the *sidra*, the txacoli white wine, and the *pintxos* (tapas) enticingly laid out on the bar counter. Bar Tximista has an enviable position on the edge of an historic square, and the barman pours the cider from head-height into a glass on the counter. It's made by Zapiain, one of the region's larger producers, and it's cool and refreshing with a lemony sharp finish. The square outside used to be the venue for bull fighting, and these days hosts a cider festival on the second Saturday in September. See the town council website, www.donostia.org for details. There are plenty of other cider bars in the city, all well worth a look, but for the best cider night out ever, get yourself out to a *sagardotegia* in the country.

Bars and producers

Sidreria El Cañu
✉ Calle del Carmen 4, Villaviciosa, Asturias 33300
📱 985 890 678

El Polesu
✉ Angel Tárano, 3, Cangas de Onís, Asturias 33550
📱 985 84 92 48

La Sifoneria
✉ San Pelayo, 28, Canas de Onís, Asturias 33550
📱 985 84 90 55

Sidra Viuda de Corsino
✉ La Riega, Nava, Asturias 33520
📱 985 71 60 67

Sidreria La Figar
✉ La Riega, Nava, Asturias 33520
📱 985 71 75 51

Sidra Roza
✉ Carretera Villabona, Nava, Asturias 33520
📱 985 71 62 02

Sidreria Barraca
✉ Calle de la Barraca, Nava, Asturias 33520
📱 985 71 69 36
🖥 www.sidreriala barraca.com

Trabanco
✉ Lugar Lavandera, Gijón, Asturias 33350
📱 985 13 80 03

Sagardotegia Gartziategi
✉ Gartziategi Baserria, Astigarraga 20115
📱 943 46 96 74
🖥 www.gartziategi.com

Bar Tximista
✉ Plaza de la Constitución, Donostia
📱 943 42 23 70

Cider Museums

Museo de la Sidra
Plaza Principe de Asturias
Nava, Asturias 33520
www.museodelasidra.com

Sagardoaren Museoa Astigarragan
Kale Nagusia 48, Astigarraga 20115
T: 943 550 575
www.sagardoetxea.com

Links

Asturias
www.sidradeasturias.es
www.sidra.com
www.infoasturias.com
www.grupotrabanco.com
www.sidrerias.com

Basque Country
www.turismoa.euskadi.net
www.gartziategi.com
www.donostia.org

France

Cider is made throughout France, but apple trees grow best where there is plenty of sunshine and buckets of rain, so northern France is where you'll most often find cider made and enjoyed. In 2007, France produced 63.7 million litres of cider, and the country consumes 13% of all cider made in Europe – the second largest market after the UK. Cider is sold in shops and supermarkets, as well as direct from the producer, but not, as a rule, in the bars and *bar-tabacs* where *biere* and *vin rouge* reign supreme. French cider is an excellent accompaniment to food, especially the soft cheeses, pancakes, seafood and *charcuterie* of the north. No surprise then that restaurants and *crêperies* are another good bet for finding traditional French cider.

Cider was well established in the Basque Country by the twelfth century, from where its production expanded northwards into Normandy. The earliest records of cidermaking in Normandy are from the thirteenth century, and from there cider spread into England and had even reached Wales by the fourteenth century. French cider is characteristically served in champagne-style bottles, this practice having been introduced in the 1960s. It usually has a rich golden colour, with a full, tannic flavour from the bitter-sweet cider apples of the region. Bottle-fermentation produces a delicate, small-bubbled mousse, and leaves a small amount of yeast sediment in the base. There would appear to be no truly dry ciders – 'they wouldn't sell!' I was told – and even those labelled *brut* are only partially fermented, perhaps to 4% abv, leaving plenty of residual sugar. Sweet ciders (*doux*) can be as low as 2% abv, and require a drinker with a particularly well-developed sweet tooth!

When in France we do of course want to avoid the industrial ciders that have had all of the flavour pasteurised and filtered out of them, and concentrate instead on the pure-juice, natural ciders. But how to distinguish them? One rule of thumb is to select bottles with a large indentation under the base, and a yeast sediment inside. Another good bet is to look for the words *Cidre Fermier* (farm cider). There is, however, only one sure-fire way of finding outstanding artisanal cider – look for the AOC (*Appelation d'Origine Contrôlée*) or PDO (Protected Designation of Origin) marks on the bottle labels. These are legal guarantees of geographical origin, traditional

Cidermaker Eric Maertens

methods of production, and quality. Three groups of cidermakers in France have these designations – the cidermakers of Cornouaille in Brittany, the perrymakers of Domfront in Normandy and the cidermakers of the Pays d'Auge.

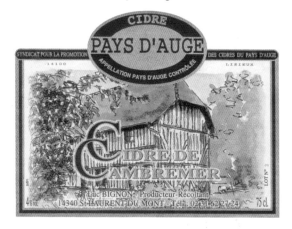

Pays d'Auge, Normandy

The Pays d'Auge has, arguably, more rustic charm than any other part of Normandy. Rolling green countryside is punctuated with standard orchards whose apple trees shelter lazy cattle. Timber-framed farms and villages are sleepy and ancient, and the bars and restaurants serve the local cider in wine glasses. The centre of this 'cider-land' is the town of Cambremer, and the local cidermakers have joined forces to offer a sign-posted *Route du Cidre* that takes you along the country lanes, from one cider farm to the next. At shops and farm-gates, look out for cider labelled *Appelation Pays d'Auge Contrôlée*.

Eric and Regine Maertens keep cows and sheep, offer holiday accommodation, and make apple juice, cider, calvados and

Grandval manor farm at Grandouet

pommeau – the region's sophisticated aperitif. 'We have 39 hectares of standard orchards, containing twelve varieties of apples,' Eric told me as we looked out over his beautiful property. 'We shake the trees with a stick, and pick the apples by hand. Then we store them in a granary where they respire water, which concentrates the flavour – the Pays d'Auge is the only region of France to use granaries like this. Without storage, one tonne of apples will give 700 litres, but after two or three weeks up in the granary the yield is down to 600 litres.'

Eric took me inside to show us his cidermaking equipment. 'After we mill the apples,' he told me, 'we let them macerate for five hours. Then

Stephane Grandval with his AOC trophy

they are pressed on our double-bed pneumatic press. The cows eat the left-over pulp, and fermentation of the juice is left to the natural yeasts. During fermentation I rack the cider off four or five times, and taste each vintage to see if it needs to be blended. Come January the mobile communal bottling plant arrives, and three people can bottle about 1000 bottles per hour.' Eric makes around 12,000 bottles of cider a season, and in April they are tasted and tested, and those that make the grade are awarded the AOC status. Those that don't are sold as the perfectly good *Cidre Fermier*. 'Now when the travelling still arrives, the whole village turns out!' he laughed, 'and it can produce 300 litres of spirit each day.' After aging it is sold as calvados, which, when blended with two parts apple juice and aged, is turned into *pommeau*.

Grandouet is a pretty village with a twelfth century church, and right beside it is the farm of Stéphane and Elisabeth Grandval. Cidermaking here is a slightly larger concern, with an annual 50,000 bottles as well as plenty of calvados and *pommeau*. At the front of the farm is an old stone mill, a timber-framed shop with a spirit still in the corner, and a barn in which you can watch an eight-minute cidermaking film in French or English. However it's around the back where the real action happens, and where modern technology is used to take the strain out of a fully traditional process. Apples are stored in palettes, and then juiced quickly with a modern pneumatic press. Fermentation happens in stainless steel vats, and the cider is bottled at a specific gravity of 1030. Stephane took me to see some huge old oak barrels, or *tonnes*, the oldest of which were dated 1792. 'The cider that is destined to become calvados is first stored for one year in these *tonnes*,' he told me, 'and after distillation is stored for either five or eight years in small 400 litre barrels.' Back in his shop I tasted his superb golden cider, all

gentle fizz on the tongue, with a long-lasting fruity-tannic finish. No wonder he's been so successful at the annual competition organised by the *Cru de Cambremer*, an organisation which recognises the best ciders in the region.

Domfront, Normandy

Down in southern Normandy, the perry pear orchards of the Domfront region must be one of the Seven Wonders of the Cider World. To see these huge trees in blossom, many of them over 300 years old, is an awe-inspiring sight that I challenge anyone not to be moved by. Orchard after orchard of these gentle giants comes into view as you drive around the perry farms, and in the medieval town of Domfront the perry itself is served chilled in champagne flutes in the bars and restaurants. The actual epicentre of perryness is not, however, Domfront,

Glass of perry at Bar Normand, Domfront

but the tiny nearby village of Mantilly, with its two quiet bars, and its bi-annual perry festival on even-numbered years, over the second weekend in July. On visiting perry farms look out for labels with the legend *AOC Poiré Domfront*.

An orchard of 80 grand old perry pear trees marks out the farm of Pascal and Marie Brunet. Marie kindly took the time to give me the grand tour, and explained that their income is from cider, jam, B&B and an annual 15,000 bottles of *poiré*. She pointed out the different varieties

Marie Brunet with some of her perry pears

of perry pear trees, naming them *Faussey, Blot, Gaubert* and *Plant Blanc.* 'Plant Blanc is the best variety we have,' she explained, 'since it has the highest sugar gravity and the best taste. In fact the AOC legislation insists that *AOC Poiré Domfront* must contain a proportion of *Plant Blanc.*'

Marie showed me into the fermentation room. 'After milling we macerate the pears for 12 to 24 hours, and then use a cloth and slat twin-bed hydraulic press. We blend juice from all four of our pear varieties, and then ferment at 4°C for a nice slow fermentation. We bottle in January when the gravity is 1030, using finings to remove most of the yeast, with the last bit providing the fizz in the bottle.' She took me back out to the orchard, and poured a glass of her perry. It was a very pale yellow with an enticing aroma, a gentle fizz, a peary medium-sweet palate, and a long classy fruity finish.

Closer to Mantilly is the farm of Jean-Claude and Louisette Fourmond-Lemorton. They were kind enough to take a break from making perry, and chatted to me as they showed me around their farm. They showed me what remained of their old orchard. The Great Storm of Boxing Day 1999 knocked down half of their 150 ancient perry pear trees, but they still consider themselves lucky, 'some people lost all of their trees'. They've planted new trees, but it'll be 30 years before they produce a significant crop. They both had grandfathers who made calvados, so they carry this tradition on, as well as making cider and an annual 5-6,000 bottles of perry. 'We do all of our picking for perry by hand,' Jean-Claude told me, 'but we use a picking machine for the calvados, since there's no need to check the degree of ripeness of the pears.' The local tradition is to use a blend of perry and cider to make calvados. 'We use 80% perry and only 20% cider, which is a higher proportion of perry than most other people.' I tried a glass of their perry, which had been made with a single variety – *Plant Blanc.* It was yellow with beads rising up the glass. As always, the taste did not disappoint, with a depth of fruity flavour in which acidity balanced the natural sweetness.

Pear juice pours from the press at Fourmond-Lemorton

Cornouaille, Brittany

Brittany clings to its Celtic roots, feeling more comfortable in the company of its sister Celtic nations than with the rest of France. Many of its pubs have an Irish theme going on, and sell the excellent local craft ales.

But down in the south, around the town of Quimper, there's a hotbed of cidermaking, with the sunny climate giving no shortage of fermentable sugars in the apples. A great place to try the cider is at the ubiquitous *crêperies* that are found throughout this region, where it is served in ceramic tea-cups, and makes a great accompaniment to both the savoury *galettes* and the sweet *crêpes*. Several cidermakers are just a short drive out of Quimper. When buying cider, keep a look out for bottles carrying the *Appellation Cornouaille Contrôlée* label.

Hervé Seznec is proud to be the fourth generation of his family to run the Cidrerie Manoir de Kinkiz. His cider cellar is something to be proud of too, a veritable cathedral of cider, with its rows of ancient oak 'foudre' barrels and stained glass windows. 'French cider cellars are always on the ground floor,' he told me, 'underground it's too cold for fermentation.' Hervé has 27 hectares of orchards, containing local Breton varieties such as *Kermenien* (a bitter variety), *Douce*

Huën (a sweet) and *Jurellin* (a sharp). 'Our AOC cider contains a blend of five to eight varieties,' he explained, 'and is a pure-juice cider. A committee come to look at my orchards, examine my apples, and taste the cider. If all is up to standard I am given just enough AOC bottle-neck labels to cover the volume of cider within each barrel given AOC status.' He gave me a welcome taster and I wasn't disappointed. Burnished gold, with a deep farmhouse apple aroma – a creamy mouthfeel gave way to a long, fruity and complex finish. Perhaps a little drier than its Norman equivalent?

I meet Guy and Anne-Marie Le Lay at their Distillerie des Menhirs, also a short drive out of Quimper. As the name suggests, they specialise in products from the distillation of cider, but sell a fine AOC cider too. Guy's father, grandfather and great-grandfather all distilled using a horse drawn itinerant still with iron wheels. Nowadays Guy has a new gas-fuelled still, and houses it in another impressive cider cellar, with row upon row of oak barrels, and a stained glass window showing the mythical apple-covered island of Avalon. Anne-Marie gave me a taste of their award-winning *AOC Pommeau de Bretagne* (17% abv), an aperitif that is served chilled. 'It is a blend of one part *lambig*, our Breton version of calvados, and three parts apple

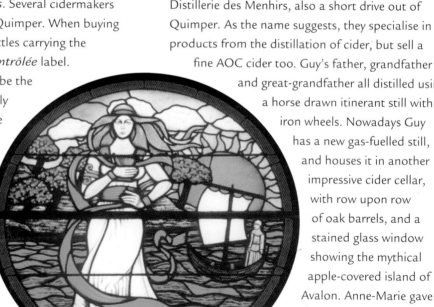

Stained glass window in Distillerie des Menhirs' cellar, showing the apple tree-covered island of Avalon

juice' she told me. It can be sold after two years ageing, but is better with more, and her four-year-old was terrific. It had a deep amber colour, a rich aroma that was all dried apples and alcohol, a rich and smooth dried apples taste, with toffee apples and a little alcohol burn at the finish.

At one point in the cellar were a couple of dozen tiny old oak barrels. I asked Anne-Marie about them. 'Each one belongs to one of the old men who fought for the Resistance during the war – as a reward they were granted licences to make *lambig*. We distil it for them, but they cannot pass the licences on, and so every year there are fewer and fewer barrels...'

Bars and producers

Eric and Regine Maertens
✉ Ferme du Lieu Roussel, Douville en Auge, Dozul
📱 02 31 23 71 15

Stéphane and Elisabeth Grandval
✉ Gaec du Manoir de Grandouet, Grandouet
📱 02 31 63 12 43

Pascal and Marie Brunet
✉ Ferme de la Prémoudière, Saint Denis de Villenette
📱 02 33 37 23 27

Jean-Claude and Louisette Fourmond-Lemorton
✉ Le Douët Gasnier, Mantilly
📱 02 33 38 71 63

Cidrerie Manoir de Kinkiz
✉ 75 Chemin de Quinquis, Ergue-Armel, Quimper
📱 02 98 90 20 57

Distillerie des Menhirs
✉ Plomelin, Quimper
📱 02 98 94 23 68

Cider Museums

Musée du Cidre de Bretagne
Ferme de Kermarzin, Route de Brest, Argol, Bretagne
T: 02 98 27 35 85
www.musee-cidre-bretagne.com

Musée du Cidre du Pays Vannetais
Le Hézo, Presqu'île de Rhuys, Bretagne
T: 02 97 26 47 40
www.museeducidre.com

Maison de la Pomme et de la Poire
La Logeraie, Barenton, Normandie
T: 02 33 59 56 22

Musée Régional du Cidre et du Calvados
Rue du Petit Versailles, Valognes, Normandie
T: 02 33 40 22 73

Accommodation

Whilst visiting the Pays d'Auge, why not stay with an English family, making and selling cider the French way? They live in a typical Norman manor farm, surrounded by its cider orchards. B&B, evening meals, caravan campsite, cider house.

Adam & Anne Bland
Lisores, 14140 Livarot, Calvados, Normandie
T: 02 31 63 42 16.

Links

General
www.idac-aoc.fr

Domfront
www.domfront.com

Pays d'Auge
www.madeinpaysdauge.com
www.cambremer.com

Cornouaille
www.cidref.fr

Austria

The Mostviertel region, in the south-west of Lower Austria will, I hope, soon be a name on every food and drink lover's lips. It boasts an amazingly rich perry culture and regional food of the highest quality – all set in an area of scenic natural beauty. The area's visual highlight comes at blossom time in late April or early May when the Moststrasse's 300,000 pear trees burst into flower.

Mostviertel derives its name from the German word for cider and perry; *Most* (pronounced 'Mosht'). It is one of the four quarters ('viertel') that make up Lower Austria and is bordered by the Danube to the north and the Vienna Woods to the east. The picture-postcard towns and villages, and imposing farmsteads that typify the region, are unbelievably well-maintained – no tumble-down sheds filled with rusty farming equipment here! Running snake-like through 200 kilometers of rolling

hills is the Moststrasse, a road that will take you to perry heaven and provide a wonderful surprise for the wine enthusiast too.

Today the region is blooming and the *Most* is treasured by the locals and enjoyed with a wine-like appreciation. In fact, the drinks are so like white wine in body, structure and array of flavour that I was forced to draw more on my knowledge of wine than on what I've learned from tasting *poire* in Normandy and the perries of Wales and England. *Most* is more delicate in flavour than some New World wines, but it has pear and apple flavours at its very centre.

Blossomtime in the Mostviertel

Mostviertel

2–300 years ago *Most* was a popular drink sold all over Austria. The nearby cities of Vienna, Linz and Wiener Neustadt brought wealth to the region via the Danube, whilst the *Industrieviertel* (industrial quarter) was quenching its thirst with *Most* in large quantities – until the arrival of bottled beer saw the end of its all-encompassing popularity.

There were over a million apple and pear trees in the region at the start of the 20th century, and *Most* was the typical drink of farm-workers. However, as Austria's economy recovered after World War 2 and incomes grew, *Most* was seen as the drink of poor people; with farmers serving their guests wine and beer as a show of wealth. *Most* culture was dangerously close to disappearing, and agricultural policies with little regard for *Most* or the landscape paid farmers to cut down the trees and plant fields of corn.

It was only as recently as the 1980s and early 90s that things began to change for the better. Enterprising individuals began to produce *Most* of high quality and to lay the foundations for *Most*

culture to return. The unique landscape of Mostviertel began to be appreciated by the department of agriculture, and more importantly by the department of tourism. Today, farmers get financial support to replant trees, and 60,000 have been planted since 1995 as part of a local project. Now there are approximately 750,000 apple and, predominantly, pear trees in the region but surprisingly no orchards. What? No orchards?!

One producer said to me 'the quality of the fruit is diminished if trees are planted in orchards' – and I thought I was a purist! In singular lines bordering the fields the perry pear trees are in peak condition, taking all the surrounding goodness for themselves without any other trees to compete with on either side. Later the *Most*-maker confessed that there are actually two orchards now in the region, 'we are experimenting with orchards to see if the fruit can produce *Most* of high quality' he told me.

The perry pioneers of the 1980s: producers Johannes Zarl, Toni Distelberger, Karl Hauer and Sepp Zeiner, took the first steps to a new economic boom, improving the quality of the *Most* and how it was marketed to the public. A distinctive looking bottle with a unique square base – representing the shape of the farmstead – was introduced along with a glass specially designed for *Most* tasting and drinking.

The Moststrasse

The 'Moststrasse' was also established during this time. The perry pioneers began to talk to producers, restaurateurs, guest houses, villages and towns, with the aim of recruiting them to a new organization as members. The 'Moststrasse' organization was formed in 2000. The members now pay fees to cover the costs of their promotional activities and the organization receives a financial boost from Europe. Things are most definitely on the up.

Euratsfeld

The guest-house of the Hochholzer family: Landhotal Gafringwirt, is in Euratsfeld, at the western end of the Moststrasse. Landhotal Gafringwirt is a 'Topwirt', a distinction awarded annually by an organisation called 'Wirtshauskultur' (Regional Gastronomy) which aims to promote high-quality regional products. The Landhotel certainly provides that, with menus featuring cream of asparagus soup, wild garlic dumplings in a rich juicy tomato sauce and a dessert of doughnut balls with cream and *Most* sorbet, and, of course, top-quality *Most*.

Alexandra and Johann Hochholzer

It is owned by Alexandra and her husband, *Mostbaron* Johann Hochholzer; who poured my first glass of *Most*; a sparkling perry by wine producer Kirchmayr, the first producer in the region to produce a sparkling *Birnen* (pear) *Most*. Kirchmayr's Birnenschaumwein (7%) is a drink of finesse; crystal clear and delicate with a light fruityness and slight sweetness. Kirchmayr is located

in the village of Weistrach and owns the biggest wine cellar in Mostviertel – the 'Meierhofkeller' underneath the big abbey of Seitenstetten.

Johann poured another, this time a *Most* he'd made; *Most* Baron Birnenmost-Cuvee (6.5%). In 2002, approximately 19 of the region's 55 producers came together as a co-operative to declare they had become rich out of *Most*. The *Mostbarons*, as they called themselves, stand as proud figureheads for the region. They work together to experiment with new products and ensure the highest quality. This *Mostbaron* blend of pears had a sweet bouquet and was refreshing, crisp and peary on the palate. In the finish a hint of earthiness could be detected.

All *Most* is made from 100% fruit with no water, no sugar and no concentrates added. The Barons' experiments are clearly paying off, if this example is anything to go by, having achieved a drink of mass appeal with no compromise on the quality and integrity of the basic ingredients.

Most *Mosts* are a blend of some of the 200 fruit varieties used in *Most* making, but a few single varietals are produced, such as the *Dorschbirne* single variety from Zeilinger in Euratsfeld, which has a light and much more familiar perry taste but with bouquets and flavours that emphasise just how wine-like perry can be.

Neuhofen/Ybbs

Mostbaron Leopold Reikersdorfer's farm and *Heurigen*; Reikersdorfer's Presshausheuriger is an excellent example of the extent to which *Most*-farmers have diversified. As well as producing *Most*, they make their own vinegar, fruit juices, chocolate and apple chips, tea (from the peel), Schnapps (from the core), honey, oils and dried fruit – all beautifully presented. The pulp from the pressing may go to feed deer for hunting or a larger producer may send it away for conversion to bio-gas.

But it is the *Most Heurigers* (perry taverns) on this and many other farms that made me swoon. The welcoming rustic *Heurigers* are without doubt the best places to sip and savour. They all have an individual character but the wooden floors, chairs, benches and beams are common amongst them all. Imagine a simple, cosy but stylish gastro-pub – on a farm – created by an owner famous for their use of local food. The *Heurigers* are not open all year round – the law allows them to open four times a year for periods of six weeks at a time. They are licensed to serve cold food, usually consisting of slices of meat and delicate homemade sheep's cheese. Look out for the *Most-Heurigen Kalender* detailing the opening and closing times or visit www.moststrasse.at or www.mostheurige.com.

oakyness allows the fruit to come through with the fleshiness you'd feel when drinking a full-bodied Semillon wine.

I was shown around the *Most* making equipment, some of the finest you'll see on a small industrial scale; 7.5 tons of fruit pressed per hour with 85% juice extracted. It is an impressive set up from which the smaller producers also benefit, as the owner bottles their products on their behalf.

One of the more interesting aspects of this process is how they get the *Most* so crystal clear. The news wasn't the best for my vegetarian ears. Before going to the fermentation tanks, gelatine (from an animal source) was added to the juice and sent into a separator. The gelatine clings to the 'cloudy' and sinks to the bottom without it entering the fermentation process, so I was told

Ferdl Most is the second biggest producer in the region. Owners Sabine and Ferdinand Litzellachner produce mainly fruit juice, but also make 200,000 litres of pear-and-apple-mix *Most*. Apfelmost: Idared, single variety, (6%) gave me an indication of just how good apple *Most* could be. It has a familiar 'cider' aroma with a hint of bananas and grapefruit. On the palate it's light and fruity with a hint of tannin.

Next up was Apfelmost Braeburn single varietal (7%). On the nose it reminded me of roasted chicken skin and brought back recollections of a fabulous Spanish Chardonnay. A silky but penetrating

(and hoped!). Enzymes are then added to speed the process up and a beautifully clear, light yellowy-green coloured drink is produced (limited to 8% alcohol).

Viehdorf

At Gasthof Sonnenhof in Viehdorf I tried more *Most* and the local '*Most* Pudding'. This drunken sponge is a must try. Before I got to desert I tasted a Lindlbirnen *Most* (6.2%) from Familie Johannes Zarl, with its 'pear drop' nose, good fruit-acidity balance and a dry finish. Following that I had Weiberleut-Most: Lebenselexier, (wife *Most* – 'for

Weiberleut-Most

Aus unbehandelten Birnen nach bäuerlicher Tradition im Fass vergoren.
6,0 Vol.% Alkohol

enthält Schwefeldioxyd

mindestens haltbar bis Ende

Lebenselexier aus dem Mostviertel

Fam. Johannes Zarl
A-3300 Amstetten, Gschirm 55
Telefon 0 74 72 / 65 425
Fax 0 74 72 / 65 425 - 4
e-mail: zarl@lieglhof.com
www.lieglhof.com

GUTES VOM LIEGLHOF

unser Karl

0,75 l 1 l

Haag

Mostheuriger Hansbauer, near Haag serves owner Hansbauer's 12-14 different varieties of *Most*.

First up was his delightful Hansbauer Birnenmost Frizzante, followed by Hansbauer Most (apple/pear blend) Gold Medal Winner and then the Pinot Grigio-esque Jonagold Apfelmost. I then sampled his Braeburn (7.6%) and finished with a couple of *Mosts* where Hansbauer had stopped the fermentation with great results. Apfelmost Florina was good but his Speckbirne (only 100 litres made) was amazing with a gentle flush of raspberries in the mouth.

On the last Sunday of April the annual festival, '*Tag des Mostes*' (*Most* Day), takes place where 50-100,000 people visit the region's *Heurigers* to sip and savour *Most*, knock back a few

The *Most* Queen

Schnapps and enjoy the local food in sunny relaxing surroundings. Attending many of the festivities is the region's *Most* Queen. The *Most* Queen is not just a pretty face. She's examined on her tasting abilities

the woman' I was told). A rich fruit nose, fuller and sweeter on the palate, with a dry finish. Johannes Zarl's Speckbirnen-Most (6.2%) came next with its Sauvignon Blanc gooseberry-like nose and well-defined structure.

There's no doubt that there are *Mosts* suitable as an aperitif, for quaffing or for sip-and-savouring, but it's with food that it shines. It's usually served in its very own wine-like *Most* glass but I also saw it served in a curvaceous pint sized glass and a half-pint glass mug.

St Peter

One of the newest *Heurigers* is owned and managed by the Binder Family – Zur Steinernen Birne. This new build certainly doesn't look like one apart from the entrance; a thirty foot pear with ironwork leaves and stem. Beautifully and sensitively constructed it was opened with much pride and in the presence of local politicians, officials, locals and me!

Mostbaron Hansbauer

and earns the right to be crowned Queen of *Most*. I was impressed to see how everyone greeted her with such warmth, joy and respect, as well as being impressed by the young lady's dedication to the job, and her ability to deliver welcomes and short speeches without any sign of nerves and always with a smile. The *Most* Queen is expected to appear at around 50 events a year and, at times, to give the royal seal of approval to each producer's *Most* quality.

Amstetten

Amstetten is one of the largest towns along the Moststrasse, and home to Most Bauernhof Distelberger. Their Speckbirner Birnenmost halbmild (6.5%), and Grüne Pichlbirn, (single variety, 6.9%) both have good structure, fruit, and were well

balanced with a mouth-watering citrus finish. The single variety Rote Pichlbirne (6.5%) reminded me somewhat of a well made but inexpensive Italian white wine, with a good steely structure, a burst of fruit and a dry finish, whilst Schweizer Wasserbirne Süß (6.3%) had elderflower on the nose and a light fruity sweetness on the palate.

Also in Amsetten is the farmstead of the ever smiling Seppelbauer, Seppelbauers Obstparadies, who specialises in Schnapps, sells fabulous sheep cheese and was willing to crack open some aged *Most* – that I was dying to try. The 17-year-old *Apfelmost* had been kept in the barrel for 6–12 months before going in the bottle for the remaining years. It was not sweet but had a depth of flavour similar to an aged

'Pear tree' at Distelberger

dessert wine. The 10-year-old Dorschbirner hadn't made the journey and was past its best. Certainly not past its best and, in my opinion, at its peak, was the 7-year-old Schweizer-Wasserbirne. Nothing explosive on the nose, but a good body with a little citrus and a strawberry finish. This is the optimum age as far as I could tell from these examples but I am open to taste others from different vintages! Another was poured – a mix of apples and pears and 20 years old. The cork floating in this cobwebbed bottle had invaded the aromas from the *Most* but it

was reasonably drinkable and oddly, the closest in flavour to that of a British cider (in a good way!) but still a long, long, way off.

A short drive takes you to the Familie Baungartner's Keller Stöckl in Amstetten. Their 6.4% Baronmost Süss & Spritzig was the first to touch my lips. A good fruity, lightly sparkling drink with tannin and a dry finish. An elegant Speckbirne (6.6%) was next with its Spanish Semillon-Chardonnay characteristics described earlier. A perfectly drinkable *Apfelmost* was followed by a Grüne Pichlbirnen, (single variety, 6.2%) with its Riesling nose and Muscat sweetness.

Normandy has always been king of the perry world in my experience – now the king has a queen. These two inspirational regions produce very different kinds of perry of the highest quality. The perry pear is the jewel in Mostviertel's gastronomic crown. Drink it, eat it, live it, and like the Austrians, make the most of it.

Bars and producers

Landhotal Gafringwirt
✉ Mittergafring 4,
3324 Euratsfeld
📱 07474 2680
🖱 www.gafringwirt.at

Reikersdorfer's Presshausheuriger
✉ Greinöd 1,
3364 Neuhofen/Ybbs
📱 07475 56481
🖱 www.mosti.at

Ferdl Most
✉ Abetzdorf 6,
3331 Kematen/Ybbs
📱 07448 2243
🖱 www.ferdl-getraenke.at

Gasthof Sonnenhof
✉ Viehdorf 13,
3322 Viehdorf
📱 07472 64198

Zur Steinernen Birne
✉ St Johann/Eng. 155,
3352 St Peter/Au
📱 07434 42112
🖱 www.steinernebirne.at

Mostheuriger Hansbauer
✉ Krottendorf 7,
3350 Haag
📱 07434 44702
🖱 www.hansbauer.at

Most Bauernhof Distelberger
✉ Gigerreith 39,
3300 Amstetten
📱 07479 7334
🖱 www.distelberger.at

Seppelbauers Obstparadies
✉ Pittersberg 12,
3300 Amstetten
📱 07472 64660
🖱 www.seppelbauer.at

Keller Stöckl
✉ Eisenreichdornach 39,
3300 Amstetten
📱 0664395 3169
🖱 www.kellerstoeckl.co.at

Cider Museums

The Most Birnhaus (Stift 9, 3300 Stift Ardagger, T: 07479 6400, www.mostbirnhaus.at) – literally the 'house of perry pears' – is a modern, bright and interactive museum, with games that represent the different stages of *Most* making and video information in bite-sized chunks.

The museum has an excellent collection of *Most* from around the region, and you can buy a glass or two (or some bottles) in the '*Mostshop*' reception area.

Germany

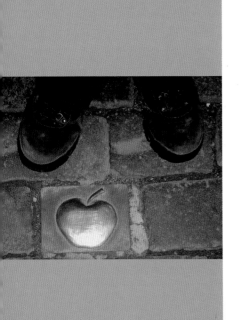

When you think of Germany, you're unlikely to think of cider. But the Viezstrasse (literally cider-street) offers a cider experience so good you'll wonder why you'd never heard of it, whilst Frankfurt, with its long tradition of *Äpfelwien* bars is Germany's undisputed cider-city central.

The Viezstrasse

The Viezstrasse is situated 135 miles south-west of Frankfurt (two hours by car) and runs along the border of Luxembourg and France; the

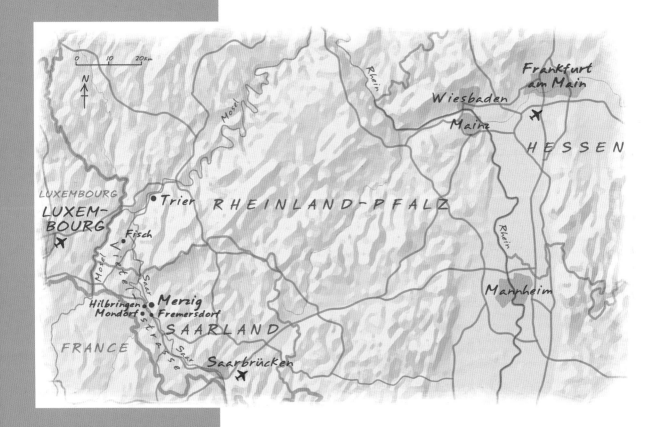

Mosel and Saar rivers providing beautiful natural boundaries on either side.

Even on the Viezstrasse it can be difficult to find traditional, pure-juice *Viez* (cider). Ordering *Viez* in a bar may result in the delivery of a commercial, light, fizzy, sweet cider, very much like the very commercial stuff that's produced in Britain. There are no short cuts here, and the only way to be certain you'll be served traditional pure-juice *Viez* is to master enough German to seek out recommendations from barkeepers and locals.

The booklet 'Gastliche Viezstrasse', available from www.tourismus.saarland.de, lists all the *Viez* bars and producers along the Viezstrasse, whilst the Viezstrasse's own website, www.viezstrasse-online.de also has maps and a comprehensive listing of *Viez*-related businesses.

Hilbringen

Crossing the Saar from the town of Merzig in the southern part of the Viezstrasse, one of the major jumping-off points for the route, it starts to feel like you are on the Viezstrasse proper as you pass apple trees and a large cider press that decorates the roadside.

The town of Hilbringen, one kilometre from Merzig, boasts an unmissable *Kelterei-Viez* (cider-press house), run by the Weitzen family –

Gasthaus Zur alten Saar. Despite the bar looking closed I tried the door and it opened into a clean, simple rural pub-restaurant where the *Viez* (pronounced 'feetz') is dispensed from a cider-press pump. This *Viez* was my benchmark and is a great example for describing the style. The traditional and best *Viez* is fresh, unfiltered, unsweetened, unpasturised and uncomplicated. It's lightly fruity without being thin and is balanced with a zing. *Viez* is usually served in restaurant-bars in its still form and is made for drinking with food. At around 5% (Weiten's was 5.5%) it only takes a couple to do the trick on an empty stomach – the 'trick' that is, is making you grasp for the menu! The Weitzen family serve a cold menu during the summer months and the food comprises of cheese dishes and cold meats accompanied by a slice or two of the world's best

***Viez* from a cider-press pump at Gasthaus Zur alten Saar**

bread – I challenge anybody and any country to put forward better bread than that produced in Germany. I was sent on my way by the generosity of a couple of local characters who insisted I drank a couple of Schnapps before heading off.

Just beyond Gasthaus Zur alten Saar, look out for their gate with a metal emblem of apples and a small orchard just beyond, marking Hilbringen as undisputed *Viez* territory.

Mondorf

Seven kilometres from Hilbringen, Mondorf is the home town of the creator of the Viezstrasse, politician Irmtraud Engeldinger. I toasted her vision and her health at Gasthaus Ginsbach, a very friendly local, with a small gathering of people sitting around the bar. The previous year had been a bad year for fruit and Gasthaus Ginsbach had been unable to make any *Viez* because of it. Fortunately enough, they were experts at making Schnapps out of any fruit available, and theirs was the best I tasted throughout my journey. Prost!

Nearby is a bar recommended as being run by a 'very old man'. Gasthaus Calmes is run by Mr Calmes. This 'old man' is the healthiest, fittest old man I've ever seen. Just seeing, let alone meeting people like him is an uplifting and inspirational experience. Nikolaus Calmes has always been barkeeper and farmer, like his father and grandfather before him. The family have occupied the property since 1850, his grandfather having built the bar onto the house in 1911. Being the easiest and cheapest drink to make for country people, every generation of the family has made

Viez. In the bar I ordered a *Viez* and he opened the cellar door on his side of the bar and disappeared. I ran around and followed him down, letting him know I was coming. Last year's bad harvest meant that I was drinking two-year-old *Viez* here. The zing had disappeared but it was still very drinkable and I thoroughly enjoyed adding the experience of tasting two-year-old *Viez* to my memory bank.

This historic old bar is a must see. It hasn't changed in generations and retains, as far as I could tell, all the original fittings, including a theatrical stage, piano and dressing room. The days of performances are now sadly over, but the stage does get used for birthdays and such like – book it now for your party!

Fremersdorf

Many of the farmhouses producing *Viez* are situated on the main roads of each town, and have either a shop or a bar attached. A tip directed me to one such *Brennerei* (distillery) in Fremersdorf, run by the Konter family. As I passed the photographic session of a local wedding, I asked an onlooker for directions. She took me to fellow onlooker Mrs Konter who took me back to her place and gave me some lovely *Viez*. The Konter *Viez* is light, almost soft-drink-like but has to be treated with respect. The shelves of their small shop were filled with an array of interestingly-designed bottles filled with Schnapps made from locally available fruit.

Fisch

In the northern region of the Viezstrasse, the town of Fisch boasts several fantastic *Viez* producers. I tentatively knocked on the door of Roland Lutz's house and was delighted to see the door swing open. Mrs Lutz greeted me with the friendliest of welcomes and within minutes I was drinking some *Viez*. Their daughter kindly provided some much needed translation as I chatted for a while. Mrs Lutz then introduced me to sparkling *Viez* – a moment I had hoped for but was not expecting this early in the journey. I'm a big fan of the sparkly cider (and perry) and the

Lutz sparkler is one of the best. In my excitement I hit tipsy and forgot to make notes, so it's down to you to get there and review it! I got to shake hands with proprietor Roland before merrily walking back up the hill to try some others.

I was greeted at the next destination, the home of Harold Wacht, by a kind-faced older lady, who waved me over to her table where she had glasses ready. The Lutz family had called ahead and told her that I was on my way.

My German was improving with every sip, and I quickly established I was in the company of Harold Wacht's mother. The *Viez* flowed and we were soon joined by Harold, his Father, his brother Otmar and Otmar's wife Ruth. The *Viez* flowed some more. We chatted for ages as Otmar and Ruth had been regular visitors to the UK and they both speak excellent English; Harold's is not bad either! We just could not stop talking cider/*Viez*. Otmar's interest in cider from Wales is genuine and passionate and was symbolised beautifully by the name he had given his touring-bike; 'Cymru'. I'd like to recommend the whole family for honorary Welsh citizenship if nobody objects.

They gave me a short tour of the area that included a truly breathtaking view of the Saar at Mettlach, and introduced me to the town's oldest

Michael Winter in his orchard

Viez Maker, Michael Winter. An hour or so later I was with Michael in his orchard looking at and biting into his German apple varieties.

After a good chat and a few shots he gave me a small flask-size bottle of Schnapps for the road. I met up with Ottmar and his wife Ruth for the evening in Saarburg where I got my first taste of Frankfurt *Äpfelwien*. Possman is possibly the biggest producer of *Äpfelwein* in Hessen, and although this enormity usually gets the warning lights flashing, I found his version of the drink much better than I'd expected – if only UK industrial producers could do this.

Trier

Trier is Germany's oldest city, founded in or before 16 BC, and is situated on the banks of the Mosel river, just north of Konz, at the north-eastern tip of the Viezstrasse.

In the suburb of Olewig, just outside the city centre lives *Viez*-maker Sven Lorscheider who sells *Viez* in bottles to take away.

Back in Trier, small craft brewery Kraft Brauerei has a lovely garden where you could happily while away several hours sitting in the sun, drinking *Viez* out of white 0.4L ceramic mugs – a fitting way to say farewell to the Viezstrasse before heading for the city.

Frankfurt

As well as being an important European financial hub, Frankfurt also has a well-established cider culture, with a long tradition of *Äpfelwein* bars. The emergence of *Äpfelwein* as a drink in the area occurred in the 1800s when a parasite wiped out all the local grapevines. The people turned to making 'wine' out of apples and consequently *Äpfelwein* has ever since been given a similar respect to that received by wine. In Frankfurt the traditional way to serve *Äpfelwein* is in a 0.3L glass but a gradual phasing out in favour for the 0.25L is underway. Prior to it being in your glass you may find it brought to your table in a large *Äpfelwein* jug.

The traditional *Äpfelwein* bars are situated south of the river Main that cuts the city in half, and there are plenty to choose from.

Äpfelwein is served with food and it's ingrained in the culture. This does however have an impact on the opening and closing times of many of the *Äpfelwein* bars, which are identified by a green wreath hanging over the doorway. Most of the bars are closed by eleven after the food-rush has passed, so if you want to get around as many as possible you'll need to start as early as possible!

Lorsbacher Thal is set back off the cobbled street. This beautiful bar, featuring a garden with grapevine canopy, is included on the newly established cider route for the Hessen region ('Hessischen Äpfelwein und Obstwiesenroute') and is a must visit. The *Äpfelwein* was fruity, light and zingy, well balanced and quaffable, coming into its own with food. There's one local dish that you must try it with; the mind-expanding *Handkäse mit Musik*, which provides an incredible cheese experience. The cheese looks like a cooked pear and is immersed in an onion dressing. It gets more challenging the more you eat but it's wonderfully intense. Make sure you shake some *kümmel* (caraway seeds) over it.

At Zum Eichkatzerl the Geiselbacher Gold *Äpfelwein* was cloudy, light and fresh, with a bit of body, rounded not zingy. The bar is a traditional classic with solid wood benches and tables, and characterful folk paintings adorn the walls of the inner bar. A full menu is available, with the *Äpfelstrudel* being particularly recommended.

Another great *Äpfelwein* bar is the Klaane Sachsehäuser. Here the *Äpfelwein* is made by the owner and is of the highest quality, this time with a hint of earthiness but leaving a clean palate. The décor is honest and genuine, with the walls of the drinking hall decorated with some great cider art; paintings, carvings and photos. Their pouring system is something special (for pouring systems that is!).

Atschel sells *Äpfelwein* by Kelterei Hoffman & Sohn. The bar bears the green wreath of the *Äpfelwein* route. The walls are adorned with the pages of a German Pomona and a single line of coat-hangers along the walls serve additionally as a decoration. Hoffman *Äpfelwein* is served – tasty and full-bodied, possibly due to the addition of apple juice. The bar's owner has a special relationship with Hoffman, making visits to the producer to select the *Äpfelwein* for his establishment, unlike other bars which tend to 'take what is delivered'.

Drei Steubern – directly opposite Zum Eichkatzerl, is a no nonsense traditional gem. The owner makes his own *Äpfelwein* and sells boiled eggs and mustard. The bar has one continuous pew around the interior and has a local, almost rural feel, despite being in the city. It's a cosy classic and the ideal venue for a good chat with friends.

Klaane Sachsehäuser's pouring system

Bars and producers

Gasthaus Zur alten Saar
✉ Zur alten Saar 20,
Merzig-Hilbringen 66663
📱 06861 2757

Gasthaus Ginsbach
✉ Silwingerstrasse 30,
Merzig-Mondorf 66663
📱 06869 224

Gasthaus Calmes
✉ Zum Kalkwerk 15,
Merzig-Mondorf 66663
📱 06869 261

Konter Brennerei
✉ Tulpenstraße 7,
Rehlingen-Fremersdorf
66780
📱 06861 77648

Roland Lutz
✉ Am Brunnen 14,
Fisch 54439
📱 06581 2836
🖰 www.viezvonlutz.de

Harold Wacht
✉ Kapellenstrasse 19,
Fisch 54439
📱 06581 4003

Sven Lorscheider
✉ Trier-Viez, Olewiger
Strasse 175, Trier-Olewig
54295
📱 0651 9930047
🖰 www.getraenke-
lorscheider.de

Kraft Brauerei
✉ Olewiger Strasse 135,
Trier 54295

Lorsbacher Thal
✉ Grosse Rittergasse
49-51, Frankfurt am Main
60595
📱 069 61 64 59
🖰 www.lorsbacherthal.de

Zum Eichkatzerl
✉ Dreieichstrasse 29,
Frankfurt am Main 60594
📱 069 61 74 80
🖰 www.eichkatzerl.de

Klaane Sachsehäuser
✉ Neuer Wall 11,
Frankfurt am Main 60594
📱 069 61 59 83
🖰 www.klaane-
sachsehaeuser.de

Atschel
✉ Wallstrasse 7,
Frankfurt am Main 60594
📱 069 61 92 01

Kelterei Hoffman & Sohn
📱 060 24 15 61
🖰 www.hoffman-
apfelwein.de

Drei Steuwern
✉ Dreieichstrasse,
Frankfurt am Main 60594

Lagerhaus
✉ Dreieichstrasse 45,
Frankfurt am Main 60594
📱 069 62 85

The *Äpfelwein* is never going to set the world alight but there's something so honest about the place – and the drink – that you can't help but love it. Served at cellar temperature it makes your mouth water and ordering another egg feels compulsory.

Restaurant Lagerhaus has been open for 10 years, selling organic *Äpfelwein*, wine, beer and meals with as many of the ingredients organic as is possible. The Matsch und Brei (translates as Mud and Mulch) *Äpfelwein* they serve is fantastic and is well worth seeking out.

Accommodation

In the northern part of the Viezstrasse, the smallest privately owned Brauhaus offers accommodation.

Mannebacher Brauhaus & Landhotel
Hauptstrasse 1a, 54441 Mannebach
T: 06581 99580
www.mannebacher.de

Links

Merzig Tourist Office
Tourismusverband Merzig-Wadern e.V.,
Poststrasse 12, 66663 Merzig
T: 06861 73874
www.merzig-wadern-online.de

Frankfurt Tourist Office
info@tcf.frankfurt.de
www.frankfurt-tourismus.de
T: 069 21 23 88 00

Ice Cider

Temperate summers, plentiful orchards and dependable sub-zero temperatures in early winter have led to the creation of this uniquely Canadian product. Pressed from the juice of apples allowed to hang on the trees until the first hard frost, ice cider is a sweet, smooth, golden-amber dessert drink, with a typical 12% abv.

Based on the German *Eiswein* tradition, ice wine production took off in Ontario in the 1970s. Ice cider was the creation of French emigré Christian Barthomeuf, an ice wine producer who, in 1989, hit upon the idea of using the same techniques he used in ice cider making with a hardier fruit: the apple. Christian now owns his own winery and ice cider orchards – Clos Saragnat, and ice cider is produced all across the Eastern Townships of Quebec, and celebrated as the area's signature drink.

As with the grapes used in ice wine making, the cider apples are left to freeze on the tree or picked and left to freeze outside, concentrating their natural sugars. The frozen apples are then pressed and the resulting juice is fermented with wine yeast for about eight months. Different ice cider makers employ their own techniques. At Domaine Pinnacle, the ice cider is blended after fermentation; other ice-cider makers blend it before. Some ice cider makers, such as La Face Cachée de la Pomme employ a less intensive method called cyroconcentration, whereby the juice of unfrozen apples is extracted and left outside to freeze over a long period before it is fermented. This range of different production methods and different ensuing results means that, if you get the chance to, it's worth sampling a few. La Face Cachée de la Pomme holds an Annual Snow Day in January when visitors can participate in the harvest and try the ciders, whilst Clos Saragnat and Domaine Pinnacle offer free cider tastings.

Ice cider is growing in popularity around the world, and producers are scooping international awards. It is currently only available in the UK through importers such as www.wineandco.com, so British cider-lovers will have to cross the Atlantic to properly sample this unique cider. For a true Quebec ice cider experience, many producers offer free tastings to visitors, alongside picnics of locally produced cheese, meats and pastries.

Bars and producers

Clos Saragnat
✉ 100 Chemin Richford, Frelighsburg, Quebec, J0J 1C0
☎ 450 298 1444
🖱 www.saragnat.com

Domaine Pinnacle
✉ 150 Chemin Richford, Frelighsburg, Quebec, J0J 1C0
☎ 450 298-1222
🖱 www.domainepinnacle.com

La Face Cachée de la Pomme
✉ 617 Rote 202, Hemmingford, Quebec, J0L 1H0
☎ 450 247-2899
🖱 www.appleicewine.com

Conservation

Introduction

Real cider and perry are long-established, multi-faceted, refreshing and invigorating drinks which everyone should be able to enjoy. However, finding real cider in your local pub can prove to be as difficult as it was to find real ale some 30 years ago.

The increasing ties of large pub companies and the loss of free houses means the number of outlets for real cider is diminishing across the nation.

The situation with real perry is even more critical as trees are not being replaced after being grubbed up and therefore the supply of perry fruit is being reduced, pushing the price up of any perry pears which are still around. Year on year, perry production is being outstripped by demand as more consumers reawaken their taste buds to this unique drink.

With multimillion pound budgets, big brands are spending a fortune on TV advertising. Many of the best-known ciders in the UK – pasteurised and filtered to remove any variations produced by the fruit – are bland, cold, fizzy keg products.

With the outlook for real cider and perry looking grim, CAMRA set up a dedicated cider and perry committee in 1988. It monitors all aspects of the industry, works with producers, runs an annual National Championship competition, a National Cider and Perry Pub of the Year Award and lobbies national and European governments. The committee also considers entrants for the coveted Pomona Award which is a prestigious accolade given to the person, place or thing which has done most for cider and perry. Much consideration and deliberation goes into each entrant and the Pomona Award is not automatically awarded annually.

And all this is in addition to promoting and informing consumers about the choice of real cider and perry which is available.

In the past five years, the number of producers has blossomed and more real cider and perry is now being produced than 15 years ago. Most of these cidermakers are hobby producers, though several are reaching the tipping point where they are able to pack their day jobs in and produce full time.

However, all is not rosy in the orchards as, in truth, old traditional orchards are becoming fewer. A wealth of diversity in both cider apples and perry pears is being lost along the way. Some producers are fighting back by celebrating this, albeit limited, diversity and creating innovative single varietal ciders, whilst others are working to preserve old varieties by founding heritage orchards of rare trees.

Consumers of real cider and perry have turned a corner. The increased number of outlets entered into CAMRA's National Cider and Perry Pub of the Year competition shows that more licensees are being turned on to the potential of offering products which do not require gas assisted pressure to be served. Conservation of the remaining orchards is vital to ensure that future generations will still be able to contemplate the origins of cider apple and perry pear names while savouring the flavour of a timeless drink. There are several organisations and campaigns dedicated to orchard conservation and bringing the pleasures of cider and perry to the wider world.

Conservation – it's everyone's issue

We can all enjoy cider and perry at the pub or beer festival, but is there more to the drink? What are its origins? Can we see the fruit from the trees or is 'Orchard Close' the name of a new housing development coming soon to an area near you?

The facts from The Department of Environment, Food and Rural Affairs (DEFRA) are that over 60 percent of the UK's own apple orchards have been grubbed up since 1970, largely as a result of EU subsidies. Indeed, between 1966 and 1995 200,000 farms have disappeared in the UK, leading to us importing 434,000 tonnes of apples in 1996, nearly half of which came from outside the EU.

This is a very worrying situation, as without the fruit it is impossible to produce cider or perry – arguably two of the UK's most environmentally green and timeless products. Enormous producers are known to routinely have fruit flown in from South Africa, New Zealand and Chile to ensure they have year round production – but for smaller producers it is the availability of local fruit which allows them to create a local product during the autumn and winter season.

CAMRA recognises the central and essential aspect of orchards to cider and perry production and has in the past five years successfully campaigned to have the Common Agricultural Policy (CAP) Reforms altered to include traditional orchards. This means that traditional orchards are now recognised by the European Union for their environmental value and are therefore eligible for a single payment under CAP making the land more likely to be retained as an orchard.

Stepping back a stage from European and government grants how did we arrive at this position? How have orchards become threatened in the first place and what is the effect of their loss on the local environment and community?

It requires a certain assiduity and vision to put land aside for the creation of an orchard. Knowledge also plays a large part. Generations ago, orchards were planted with a sufficient mix of bitter-sweet and bitter-sharp trees to produce the perfect balanced product when the fruits were pressed and fermented together. This reveals the forward planning skill of producers who were looking to the resultant drink even as they planted.

However, knowledge of fruit types is being lost as we move into a homogeneous situation where fruit is now mainly purchased from supermarkets. In 2005, Friends of the Earth noted that at the height of the UK apple season around two thirds of the apples on sale in supermarkets were imported. While some supermarkets have tried to assure consumers they do source local apples, in the majority of cases you will find apples which are possibly more widely travelled that yourself. Organisations like Brogdale and the Marchers Group regularly arrange fruit identification days to assist orchard owners in discovering what fruit they are actually growing – information that is essential as the genetic pool of varieties continues to dwindle.

Brogdale in Faversham, Kent is home to the National Fruit Collections and has the largest collection of varieties of fruit trees in the world. Over 2,300 different varieties of apple, 550 of pear, 350 of plum, 220 of cherry, 320 varieties of bush fruits, as well as smaller collections of nuts & vines are grown here, in 150 acres of beautiful orchards. Spectacular in blossom time, the orchards are also at their best in late summer & autumn. Brodgdale runs events through the year with the emphasis on education and diversity.

Once established, the orchard needs to weather the constantly changing farming grant structures where priorities change over time and generations without any formal protection other then the landowners enjoyment of the product itself. Strange though it may seem, perry pear trees which can be over 300 years old generally do not have tree protection orders attached to them – which means that the tree can be removed or chopped down at the whim of the landowner. Indeed the tree is ascribed no intrinsic value from a planning point of view as it's the land alone which has the value attached to it. Fortunately, many organisations work to preserve our orchard heritage.

Common Ground and the concept of Local Distinctiveness appear to have been around for ages but was only in 1990 that Common Ground launched Apple Day at a blustery Covent Garden alongside some notable CAMRA volunteers. Common Ground is a resource to signpost and lead you through activities and options – a bit like a virtual community resource for the earth.

Across the UK, three Regional Producers Associations exist – one in Wales, one in the South West, and one in the Three Counties. They wield an impressive span of expertise and influence.

Since the 1980s, the Slow Food movement has become an international organisation of 80,000 members in 90 countries who not only care about enjoying and retaining our diverse heritage of regional food and drink and protecting it from globalisation, but are increasingly aware of the associated environmental issues. Slow Food have created a virtual Ark of food and drink products that were steeped in local heritage and under threat. Because of the efforts of an initially small group of perry producers, the Three Counties Perry Presidium was formed and given its rightful place within the Ark. It is said perry thrives within the sight of May Hill in Gloucestershire and, as the results of CAMRA's National Champion Perry Awards show, this is still generally where award-winning perries hale from.

A unique National Collection of Perry Pears exists at the Three Counties Showground, which is also the host venue to two impressive farming and food fairs each year which celebrate and delight in local perry and cider. These are well worth attending as you get to meet producers face to face and sample products which sometimes are not widely available.

Sustain, another innovative and groundbreaking conservation group, advocates food and agriculture policies and practices that enhance the health and welfare of people and animals, improves the working and living environment, promotes equity and seeks to enrich society and culture. Their recent publication 'Protecting Our Orchard Heritage' is a good practise guide for managing orchard projects and is essential reading and reference material for anyone thinking of conserving orchards.

These and other organisations are well placed to meet any future challenges to orchards swiftly and positively. CAMRA is happy to continue working with them to ensure future supplies of the cider and perry.

Brogdale in Faversham, Kent has the largest collection of varieties of fruit trees in the world

Pomona Awards

The Pomona Award is named after the Roman Goddess of apples, and is presented by CAMRA to the person, people, place or thing who has done the most to promote real cider or perry over the previous 12 months or for ongoing work.

2008

Roger Wilkins, Wilkins Cider

A Somerset-based farmhouse cidermaker who learnt his trade at his grandfather's knee. Roger has been making cider since 1969, and wining CAMRA awards since the 1980's. A unique and dedicated individual with a passion for his products that is hard to equal.

2007

The Big Apple Organising Committee

A Herefordshire-based group dedicated to promoting English orchards, apples and cider. They earned the Pomona Award for their unflagging support and involvement with real cider and perry by hosting their annual Blossom Time and Harvest Time feativals.

2006

Joint Award to:
Jon Hallam and John Reeks

Both wholesalers were jointly awarded the accolade for supplying pubs and beer festivals with a range which would not otherwise be obtainable, and encouraging farmers to continue producing cider and perry.

2005

Ivor and Susie Dunkerton, Dunkertons Cider Co.

Ivor and Susie Dunkerton were the first Soil Association certified organic producers in Herefordshire. They were given the award for their tireless work since 1979 in establishing cider and perry as a premium product, and for their extensive orcharding work.

2003

Cymdeithas Perai Seidr Cymru (Welsh Perry and Cider Society)

The society way founded in 2001 to support Welsh-produced craft cider and perry. They were commended for raising the profile of Welsh Cider and Perry, arranging an annual competition for Welsh producers, encouraging the planting of trees, identifying old varieties, and ensuring that more pubs choose to sell real cider and perry.

2002

Paul Johnson, Johnson's Farmhouse Cider

Cider producer on the Isle of Sheppy making blended cider and cider from his own orchard. He gained the award for having the vision to plant an orchard of more than 50 standard cider apple trees with a dozen different varieties.

2001

Rod Marsh, The National Collection of Cider and Perry

The manager of the National Collection of Cider and Perry – a unique celebration of our national fruit. However, Rod Marsh declined the award stating 'My own contribution to cider in the UK is in its infancy compared to those whose families have striven to make out national beverage through several generations... We need to wake up as a nation and appreciate what we have.'

1999

Kevin Minchew, Minchew's Real Cyder & Perry

Producer dedicated to sourcing, growing and making cider and perry from historic tree varieties. He was commended for his dedication to tracing old varieties of cider and perry fruit, often thought lost, and ensuring that they continue to be celebrated and enjoyed as real cider and perry.

1998

Gerry Alton, Brogdale

Gerry established Brogdale as home to the National Fruit Collections: a genetic pool of cider and perry fruit providing an excellent service for both growers and producers.

Common Ground

Common Ground
APPLE DAY OCTOBER 21st

Common Ground champions popular involvement with nature and promotes celebration as the starting point for local action to improve the quality of ordinary places and everyday lives. The originators of Apple Day, Common Ground are also committed to preserving and creating orchards, and their Community Orchards scheme aims to create orchards of fruit trees that are owned by and freely accessible to the communities which found and maintain them. More information about Common Ground can be found on their websites www.commonground.org.uk and www.england-in-particular.info.

Orchards make cider, cider makes orchards

Orchards of tall trees show that we can have it all – good food and fine drink, wild creatures, a healthy ecosystem and beautiful surroundings. Culture and nature intertwining so well that there is room for both and richness in each. The orchard has a symbolic value as a messenger of possibility and hope in difficult times.

Common Ground encourages people to actively create a new relationship with nature, starting in their own neighbourhood. What better than an orchard revival: trees in gardens can become the orchards that hold the suburbs together, orchards can become the heart of villages. Fruit trees in the smallholdings colonising the green belt, espaliered trees growing against the walls of the city, roofs sprouting with coppiced nut trees, fruit corners in parks and around workplaces, linear orchards along railways and canals, wild fruit in hedgerows –

Traditional cider orchards in Somerset

all are orchards linking town and country, place with place, people with nature.

Costermongers sold apples (costards) in the streets – would that they were still crying their wares. But the bald truth is that we have let our rich cider and apple inheritance slip through our fingers. At the height of our long season, apples from the other side of the world, stifled by carbon dioxide to suspend their ripening, are sold on superstore shelves. We import over 70% of our apples. And the cider cobbled together from imported concentrate disgraces our cider heritage. We have let ourselves be so deskilled that we cannot even name more than a few varieties of apple and hardly any pears, plums, damsons, cherries, walnuts or hazelnuts. The recipes passed down for different apples and fruit across the season have faded away.

Worse, the orchards themselves have fallen or been felled. 63% of England's orchards have been lost since 1950. The decline of traditional fruits and orchards, in which we are all implicated, has denuded every county, city, town and village of the trees that in blossom would bring insects, in leaf would give shade, in fruit would lure birds and in winter light might sport mistletoe; which across the year would give glamour and particularity to the scene.

Within Britain, many an apple has a long history and intriguing story to tell that locates it in place, embossing it with local identity: Newton Wonder was found growing in the thatch of a Derbyshire pub; Yarlington Mill named for the waterwheel in Somerset where it was discovered. Their names alone are enough to beguile us: Catshead, Dogsnout,

Forty Shilling, Hoary Morning, Roundway Magnum Bonum – descriptive, evocative, imaginative. Isaac Newton's Tree; Laxton's Triumph; Peacemaker – suggesting stories to be discovered and told. Crawley Beauty, Devonshire Quarrendon, Kentish Fillbasket, Keswick Codlin, Lass O' Gowrie, Norfolk Biffin, Yorkshire Greening – implicating places of origin. Benenden Early, Hambledon Deux Ans, May Queen – claiming seasons of eating and qualities of keeping. And then the cider apples.... Brown Snout, Captain Broad, Dabinett, Fillbarrel, Foxwhelp, Kingston Black, Pocket Apple, Slack ma Girdle, Sweet Coppin, Ten Commandments – particular to the southwestern and Severnside counties.

Planting pips is something children do, but it is also the pastime of farmers and cider makers, horticulturalists and research station white coats eager to see what new potential will arise. Some keep a strong eye on parentage. Some spread the must from cider making around the field edge and select interesting trees that arise years later to fruit, perchance to make a fortune. Perhaps the greatest democratic experiment has happened along lanes, railways and roadside verges. Far flung apple cores – the seeds escaping devouring insects, moulds and mammals – have grown to blossom and bring bright autumn apples that sometimes cling until spring. Un-researched, there may be future market leaders out there waiting to be discovered and named.

Growing trees is one thing, making cider is another and there are examples of people getting together to do both. Since 1992, when Common Ground put forward the idea of Community Orchards, hundreds have been established throughout the country. These orchards are various and variegated. There is no single pattern – groups are finding ways of looking after them that best suit their own requirements.

We need more places where we can relax, play, work and learn. We need shared activities to enable people of different ages and backgrounds to come together. We need places where we can be enlivened by nature working with us. In city, town or village, the Community Orchard is becoming a communal asset for the whole parish. More than that, it can be the focal point – the moot, or open-air community hall. Orchards can work in housing estates and industrial estates, in hospital and school grounds, in city and suburb, village and market town. They can help us improve our diet, offer healthy activity, enliven a curriculum and help to speed the recovery of the sick.

At a time of unprecedented alienation from nature and understanding about where our food comes from, Community Orchards are reviving interest in fruit growing – sharing knowledge and horticultural skills, pressing juice and making cider as a social activity. In the face of climate change, the need to reduce food miles makes the provision of locally grown food and drink ever more urgent.

Community Orchards can offer places for quiet contemplation and centres for local festivities. They act as carbon sinks, reservoirs for local varieties of fruit and refuges for all manner of wildlife. Community Orchards can reinforce local distinctiveness, as people band together to save vulnerable old apple, pear, cherry, damson and plum orchards; plant anew to help to counteract the loss of local varieties of fruit; or experiment in a warming climate by planting apricots, almonds and olives.

They may be owned or leased by a community group, voluntary organisation, parish council or other tier of local authority. Local people can share the orchard harvest or profit from the sale of its produce, taking responsibility for any work to be done. They could be part of a chain that links the playing field or recreation ground with the common, the park, the local nature reserve, disused quarry, allotments and churchyard. Too few orchards have been planted in parks and landscape schemes. But there are exceptions that we hope will start a trend: in Darenth Country Park, Dartford, Kent in 2000, 150 standard trees and about 50 semi-dwarf fruit trees were planted. And in Brocks Hill Country Park, Oadby, Leicestershire, 172 mixed fruit trees were planted as a Community Orchard.

Ours has been a campaign to help people to change for the better the way we live in the world. We conceived Apple Day (October 21st) and Community Orchards as ways of prompting social activity, celebrating and demonstrating that variety and richness matter to a locality. In linking particular apples and other fruits with their place of origin, we hope that orchards will be increasingly recognised and conserved for their contribution to local distinctiveness including the rich diversity of wildlife and culture they support.

After 20 years of championing orchards we recognise that we have started to make a difference in how people think and in how they act, but the counter-forces are immense – climate change, global and local economics, ignorance, complacency, and fear of the future.

But what better demonstration that we can live well with nature do we need? An old orchard may support over 1800 species, it can feed us and help us to make fine cider, it can lift our spirits as the seasons change. Orchards offer a wise way of sharing the land – a positive gift to those who follow.

A Curious Drink for a Slow World

In 2002, John Fleming of the local Slow Food convivium approached perry producers about the possibility of support for perry from The Slow Food Foundation for Biodiversity. This manifested itself in the launch, at The Ludlow Food Festival 2004, of the Three Counties Perry Presidium, and the inclusion of perry in The Ark of Taste – a project to rediscover, catalogue, describe and publicise forgotten flavours.

Slow Food Presidia are regional projects whose goal is to help guarantee a viable future for artisan food and drink by defining production techniques, establishing production standards and promoting consumer awareness and consumption. The Ark of Taste lists products that are in danger of disappearing.

> **The Ark of Taste – a project to rediscover, catalogue, describe and publicise forgotten flavours**

Real perry – a little-known drink, from a specific area of the Three Counties of Gloucestershire, Herefordshire, Worcestershire and the Welsh Marches; made by a diminishing number of small producers from an ever dwindling number of perry pear trees – seemed a perfect fit for the support of Slow Food and for Presidium status.

The aims of the Presidium are threefold: to raise awareness of perry amongst consumers in the UK and abroad, to safeguard biodiversity, and to maintain, protect and enhance the skills involved in the production and marketing of perry.

A production protocol was produced in 2006, after a lengthy collaboration between all interested parties. This defines production techniques and standards while providing encouragement for new perry initiatives. Membership of Three Counties Perry is open to any producer in the defined geographical area, but they must make perry in accordance to the protocol and should be prepared to actively promote perry.

Three Counties Perry has attended the Salone del Gusto and Terra Madre in Turin in 2004, 2006 and 2008. The Terra Madre invites more than 5000 artisan food producers to meet during the Salone, the world's biggest artisan food fair in Turin, Italy. These two very dynamic, inspiring events bring together some of the most passionate and skilful food producers from around the world.

The Presidium is also involved at Slow Food markets in Bristol and London, as well as providing perry for local convivial dinners and events. Talks and tastings are organised as well as walks around the National Collections.

Through a time of increased awareness of local food and drink, perry has become increasingly available, especially through CAMRA festivals and wholesalers. Its popularity is such that there is now a shortage of the only raw material for making real perry: perry pears.

This is why Three Counties Perry is also engaged in support of the National Collections of Perry Pear Trees at The Three Counties showground and in Hartpury. Charles Martell created the collection at Malvern and Jim Chapman is behind the Orchard centre at Hartpury. They provide the required resource of bud and graft wood for new plantings and it is with great heart that we see a number of substantial, small and single plantings taking place.

Slow Food has taken perry to its heart and provided those producers who wish to be involved with a forum to take perry to a wider audience. The perry revival is here to stay!

Museum Orchards

Museum Orchards play an important part in cataloguing and preserving the UK's cider apple heritage. There have been many collections of cider apples: most of the old family cider businesses had mother or museum orchards to preserve their growing stock. However, many of these collections have been lost and consequently hundreds of cider apple varieties have disappeared forever and are now just names in an old tome.

Tidnor Wood Orchards CIC (Community Interest Company) farms 26 acres of orchard on the outskirts of Hereford City. The five acre Museum Orchard is home to a National Collection of '*Malus* – cider making' – genuine cider apple varieties and other varieties that have been used historically in cider making, with over 400 different apples sourced from all over the UK, the Channel Islands and Eire. This orchard is so comprehensive that they are having trouble in finding any more varieties to stock. Hopefully, this collection will provide a valuable resource for cidermakers of the future.

If England is the princess of cider making then France is the queen, but her – even more numerous – varieties are fast disappearing too. Tidnor Wood has captured ten beautiful acres near Vire in Calvados, Normandie, 'Les Vergers Tallevende', so that Egyptia, Faro, Grise Dieppois, Rambault and Tête de Brebis should be safe for future generations too.

The incorporating of the orchards into a CIC has created an 'asset lock' which means that Tidnor Wood's assets cannot be dispersed other than to another CIC or a registered charity. In this way the company hopes to preserve the orchards for the benefit of future generations. Billy Down Pippin, Camelot, Cap of Liberty, Morgan Sweet, Paignton Marigold, Shepperdine Silt, Silver Cup and others have been preserved.

To guarantee self-sustainability, Tidnor Wood is investing in 'bolt-on' activities and businesses. They have a tree sponsorship scheme, a new Victorian cider house currently awaits a cider maker, a gene bank awaits a nurseryman, and their old stone mill needs a sponsor with vision. Fully organic under the auspices of the Soil Association, Tidnor has a contract to sell all their organic fruit to Westons, which allows the orchard to be self-sufficient – not seeking grants or subsidies or other forms of charity.

Mistletoe

Mistletoe has had a long association with cider and is a distinctive feature of many traditional cider orchards in the West Country, where this unusual evergreen tree parasite grows in quantity. Apple trees (eating or cider) are its favourite host, and it thrives in the open-space habitat provided by orchards. It is curiously absent from apple orchards further east, north and south, and is generally scarce on any host trees outside Herefordshire, Worcestershire, Gloucestershire and Somerset. It is also fairly rare on pear trees.

It is rarely tolerated in modern intensive orchards because, being a parasite, it will reduce apple yield. In traditional orchards the management custom is to prune mistletoe clumps in winter, as it is much easier to see it and the female prunings, with their pearly-white berries, can be sold on as an extra crop at Christmas.

These winter mistletoe sales probably only became economically viable from the 19th century onwards, when numerous old regional midwinter mistletoe customs were slowly standardised as our modern 'kissing' custom and created a growing demand for cut mistletoe across the whole country in Christmas week.

These traditions alone make mistletoe in traditional orchards very significant in cultural conservation terms. It is worth noting that mistletoe on other 'favoured' hosts – mostly limes, poplars and willows – is not easily accessible as these trees are much too tall. Only traditional orchards can provide a ready supply of Christmas mistletoe!

Mistletoe is important from the biodiversity point of view too. It provides winter shelter for many invertebrate species; the sticky-white berries are valuable winter food for several mistletoe-specialist birds (including the Mistle Thrush); and it is the only food plant for at least six specialist mistletoe-eating insects. These include beetles, bugs and one moth and all are classified as nationally rare. The moth, known as the Mistletoe Marble Moth, was recently 'upgraded' to a Priority Species in the UK's Biodiversity Plan. Mistletoe is the essential basis of a unique mini-ecosystem.

Active management of mistletoe is necessary if we are to keep a balance between apple fruit yield, growth of mistletoe for a Christmas crop and help maximise orchard biodiversity. Some recent trends in neglected orchards, where mistletoe has been left uncropped, or where only female mistletoe has been cut, leaving the berryless male plants uncropped, have been worrying conservation groups. There is a real risk that the apple trees will eventually become overgrown and overstressed by the mistletoe, resulting in the death of host and parasite. Recent initiatives are beginning to help by demonstrating the need for ongoing management. Another need we must not forget is the inclusion of new mistletoe colonies (plant your mistletoe seeds in February) in newly-established traditional-style orchards.

Cider Library

The **Marcher Apple Network** (MAN) was founded in 1993 to try and rescue and preserve the apple heritage of the Welsh Marches. Cider fruit dominates the orchards of this area, but housing development and farmers' needs to replant to the modern type cordon orchards have contributed to the destruction of many of the old standard orchards. In the ones that still exist many of the ancient trees are neglected and dying.

It is imperative that the old varieties of cider fruit are preserved for future generations. MAN has had some success finding and grafting several varieties that were though to be 'lost'.

To bring old and lesser-known apple varieties to the attention of the general public, MAN puts on apple displays at several of the various Apple Days throughout the Welsh Marches area. Identification of specimens brought in by members of the public is also carried out, and advice offered when needed.

MAN has also produced two reference CDs – 'Herefordshire Pomona' and 'Vintage Fruit'. These contain useful information regarding the characteristics of the fruit listed including, for some, the virtue of the cider they will produce. Like a museum orchard, the information that MAN is collating will keep alive knowledge that might otherwise be lost, as a resource for current and future cidermakers.

'Nehou' cider apple

Appendices

Cidermakers with Bars, Shops, and Visitor Centres

In the old days, most cider farms would make 'farm gate' sales in quantities of five gallons or more. Legally, this counted as wholesale, so the farm didn't need an off-licence. But then the 2003 Licensing Act redefined 'wholesale' as sales to the trade, not to the general public, so farm gate sales are now a rarity.

However, many cidermakers, especially in tourist areas, now have shops, bars, restaurants, visitor centres and even museums where cider-lovers can stock up. The shops often carry a wide range of other local produce as well as cider, so if you're visiting from a less-favoured region, an estate car or even a people-carrier might be advisable.

I must offer a warning, though. The list below is far from exhaustive; so apologies to any cidermakers whose shops have been left out, or whose shops have opened since it was compiled. By the same token, it may be that some of the ventures on the list have closed by the time you read it. And as in many cases the shops are not open year-round (and when they are, they often keep distinctly erratic hours), phoning ahead is more than just a good idea.

Cornwall

Cornish Cyder Farm, Penhallow, TR4 9LW. T: 01872 573356. Tours, museum, shop, licensed restaurant.
Cornish Orchards, Westnorth Manor Farm, Duloe, PL14 4PW. T: 01503 269007. Shop.
Lizard Wine & Cider, Hirvan Lane, Predannack, TR12 7AU. T: 01326 241481. Shop.

Devon

Brimblecombe's, Farrants Farm, Dunsford, EX6 7BA. T: 01647 352783. Shop.
Countryman Cider, Felldownhead, Milton Abbot, PL19 0QR. T: 01822 870226. Shop.

Green Valley Cider, Darts Farm, Clyst St George, EX3 0QH. T: 01392 876658. Shop.
Killerton Estate Cider, Killerton House, Broadclyst, Exeter, EX5 3LE. T: 01392 881418. Shop.
Lyme Bay Winery, Shute, Axminster, EX13 7PW. T: 01297 551355. Shop.
Mill Top, Great Close, Combteignhead, Newton Abbot, TQ12 4RE. T: 01626 873291. Site is licensed.
Palmershayes Cider Farm, Calverleigh, Tiverton, EX16 8BA. T: 01884 254579. Shop.
Winkleigh Cider Co, Western Barn, Hatherleigh Road, Winkleigh, EX19 8AP. T: 01837 83560. Shop.

Glamorgan

Gower Heritage Centre, Parkmill, Gower, SA3 2EN. T: 01792 371206. Shop.

Gloucestershire

Crooked End Farm, Ruardean, GL17 9XF. T: 01594 544482. Shop.
Harechurch Cider, White Lodge, Springfields, Drybrook, GL17 9BW. T: 01594 541738. Shop.
Hayles Fruit Farm, Hailes, Winchcombe, GL54 5PB. T: 01242 602123. Shop.
Prinknash Abbey, Cranham, GL4 8EX. T: 01452 812455. Shop.
Riddle's, Oak Farm, Oldbury Lane, Thornbury, BS35 1RD. T: 01454 202839. Shop.

Hampshire

New Forest Cider, Pound Lane, Burley, BH24 4ED. T: 01425 403598. Shop.

Herefordshire

Butford Organics, Bowley Lane, Bodenham, HR1 3LG. T: 01568 797195. Shop.
Dunkerton's, Luntley, Pembridge, HR6 9ED. T: 01544 388653. Shop.
Gwatkins, Moorhampton Farm, Abbey Dore, HR2 0AL. T: 01981 550258. Shop.
Ross-on-Wye Cider & Perry, Broome Farm, Peterstow, HR9 6QG. T: 01989 769556. Site is licensed, restaurant (evenings).

Isle of Wight

Godshill Cider, High St, Godshill, PO38 3HZ. T: 01983 840680. Shop.
Rosemary Vineyard, Smallbrook Lane, Ryde, PO33 2UX. T: 01983 811084. Shop.

Kent

Badgers Hill Farm, Chilham, CT4 8BW. T: 01227 730573. Shop.

Biddenden Vineyards, Gribble Bridge Lane, Biddenden, TN27 8DF. T: 01580 291726. Shop.

Double Vision Cider, Marlpit Farm, Wierton Rd, Boughton Monchelsea, ME17 4JW. T: 01622 746633. Shop.

KS Jordan, Neals Place Farm, Neals Place Rd, Canterbury, CT2 8HX. T: 01227 765632. Shop.

Rough Old Wife, Cork Farm, Hawkin's Rough Orchard, Old Wives Lees, Canterbury, CT4 8BN. T: 07768 364353. Shop, mail order and cider-making courses

Norfolk

Norfolk Cider, The Apple Shop, Wroxham Barns, Hoveton, NR12 8QU. T: 01603 783040. Shop.

Old Chimneys Brewery, Hopton End Farm, Church Rd, Market Weston, IP22 2NX. T: 01359 221013. Shop.

Whin Hill Cider, Stearman's Yard, Wells-next-the-Sea, NR23 1BT. T: 01328 711033. Shop.

Northamptonshire

Windmill Vineyard, Windmill Hill Farm, Hellidon, NN11 6HZ. T: 01327 262023. Shop.

Oxfordshire

Upton Cider, High St, Upton, OX11 9JE. T: 01235 850808. Shop.

Powys

Ralph's Cider, Old Badland Farm, New Radnor, LD8 2TG. T: 01544 350304. Bar, shop, mail order.

Shropshire

Mahorall Farm Cider, Nash, Ludlow, S78 3AH. T: 01584 890296. Shop.

Somerset

Avalon Vineyard, The Drove, East Pennard, BA4 6UA. T: 01749 860393. Shop.

Bridge Farm Cider, East Chinnock, BA22 9EA. T: 01935 862387. Shop.

Broadlands Fruit Farm, Box Rd, Bath, BA1 7LR. T: 01225 859780. Shop.

Broadoak Cider, Clutton Hill Farm, King lane, Clutton, BS39 5QQ. T: 01275 333154. Shop.

Burrow Hill Cider, Kingsbury, TA12 5BU. T: 01460 240782. Shop.

Derrick's, Cheddar valley Cheese Depot, Cheddar, BS27 3QE. T: 01934 743113. Shop.

Dobunni Farm Cider, Wick Rd, Lympsham, BS24 0HA. T: 01278 751593. Shop.

Heck's, 9–11 Middle Leigh, Street, BA16 0LB. T: 01458 442367. Shop.

Henry's Farmhouse Scrumpy, Tanpits Farm, Bathpool, TA2 8BZ. T: 01823 270663. Shop.

Parson's Choice Cider, Parsonage Farm, West Lyng, TA3 5AP. T: 01823 490978. Shop.

Perry Bros, Dowlish Wake, Ilminster, TA19 0NY. T: 01460 55195. Shop, museum.

Rich's, Mill Farm, Watchfield, TA9 4RD. 01278 783651. Shop.

Sheppy's, Bradford-on-Tone, TA4 1ER. T: 01823 461233. Shop, visitor centre, museum.

Thatchers, Myrtle Farm, Sandford, BS25 5RA. T: 01934 822862. Shop.

Torre Farm, Washford, TA23 0LA. T: 01984 64004. Shop, tearoom.

West Croft Cider, Brent Knoll, TA9 4BE. T: 01278 760762. Shop.

Wilkins, Land's End Farm, Mudgley, BS28 4TU. T: 01934 712385. Shop.

Suffolk

Shawsgate Vineyard, Badingham Rd, Framlingham, IP13 9HZ. T: 01728 724060. Shop.

Suffolk Apple Juice, Cherry Tree Farm, Ilketshall St Lawrence, NR34 8LB. T: 01986 781353. Shop.

Sussex

Appledram Cider, Pump Bottom Farm, Birdham Rd, Apuldram, PO20 7EH. T: 01243 773828. Shop, restaurant.

Battle Cider, Burnt House Farm, Burwash Weald, TN19 7LA. T: 01424 429588. Shop.

Sedlescombe Organic Vineyard, Hawkhurst Rd, Sedlescombe, TN32 5SA. T: 01580 830715. Shop.

West Midlands

Hamstead Brewing Centre, 37 Newton Rd, Great Barr, B43 6AD. T: 0121 358 6800. Shop, mail order.

Wiltshire

Thornham Farm Shop, Great Thornham Farm, Seend, SN12 6PN. T: 01380 828295. Shop.

Worcestershire

Barnfield Cider Mill, Broadway Rd, Broadway, WR12 7HB. T: 01386 853145. Shop, café, museum.

Fernihough's Cider, Worcester Rd, Boraston, WR15 8LL. T: 01584 819632. Shop.

Knight's, Crumpton Oaks Farm, Storridge, WR13 5HP. T: 01684 568887. Shop.

Cidermakers

Contact details for the cider and perry producers mentioned in this book.

Three Counties

Brooke Farm Cider
Brook Farm, Wigmore, Herefordshire,
HR6 9UJ
T: 01568 770562
www.brookfarmcider.co.uk

Butford Organics
Bowley Lane, Bodenham,
Herefordshire, HR1 3LG
T: 01568 797195
www.butfordorganics.co.uk

Dunkertons
Pembridge, Leominster, Herefordshire
HR6 9ED
T: 01544 388653
www.dunkertons.co.uk

Gregg's Pit Cider & Perry
Much Marcle, Herefordshire,
HR8 2NL
T: 01531 660687
www.greggs-pit.co.uk

Gwatkin Cider
Moorhampton Park Farm,
Abbey Dore, Hereford, HR2 0AL
T: 01981 550258

Hartland's Cider
Tirley Villa, Tirley, Gloucester,
Gloucestershire, GL19 4HA
T: 01452 780480

Henney's
Willow Cottage, Filly Brook,
Bishops Frome, Herefordshire,
WR6 5BY
www.henneys.co.uk

King Offa Distillery
21 Ryelands Street, Hereford,
Herefordshire, HR4 0LW
T: 01432 354207
www.cidermuseum.co.uk/
OffaDistillery.htm

Ledbury Cider & Perry
Old Kennels Farm, Bromyard Road,
Ledbury, HR8 1LG
T: 01531 635024
www.ledburycider.co.uk

Lyne Down Cider & Perry
Lyne Down Farm, Much Marcle,
Ledbury, Herefordshire, HR8 2NT
T: 07756 108501
www.lynedowncider.co.uk

Newton Court Cidery
Newton Court, Leominster,
Herefordshire, HR6 0PF
T: 01568 611721

The Orgasmic Cider Company
Great Parton, Eardisley, Hereford,
HR3 6NX
T: 01544 327244

Summers' Cider and Perry
Slimbridge Lane, Halmore, Berkeley,
Gloucestershire, GL13 9HH
T: 01453 811218

Westons Cider
The Bounds, Much Marcle,
Herefordshire, HR8 2NQ
T: 01531 660233
www.westons-cider.co.uk

Wales

Gwynt y Ddraig
Llest Farm, Llantwit Fardre,
Pontypridd, Rhondda Cynon Taff,
CF38 2PW
T: 01443 209 852
www.gwyntcider.com

Ralph's Cider & Perry
Old Badland, New Radnor, Presteigne,
Powys, LD8 2TG
T: 01544 350304
www.ralphscider.co.uk

Rumsey Cider
Gellirhyd Farm, Llangenny,
Crickhowell, Powys, NP8 1HF
T: 01873 810466

Seidr Dai
91 Black Oak Rd, Cyncoed, Cardiff,
Wales CF23 6QW
T: 029 2075 8193

Seidr ô Sir
Y Betws, Betws Diserth, Powys,
LD1 5RP
T: 01982 570404

Springfield Cider
Springfield Farmhouse, Llangovan,
Monmouthshire, NP25 4BU
T: 01291 691018
www.springfieldcider.co.uk

Robert Fitchett, owner of Upton Cider,
Oxfordshire

Toloja
Ty Gwyn, Dihewyd, Lampeter,
Ceredigion, SA48 7PP
T: 01570471295
www.toloja.com

Towy Valley Cider
Llwynhaf Farm, Llanddarog Road,
Carmarthen, Dyfed, SA32 8AR
T: 01267 275509

Troggi Seidr
Lower House Cottage, Earlswood,
Monmouthshire
T: 01291 650653

WM Watkins & Sons
Ty Bryn, Upper House Farm,
Grosmont, Monmouthshire, NP7 8LA
T: 01873 821237

South West

Ashridge Cider
Barkingdon Farm, Staverton, Totnes,
Devon, TQ9 6AN
T: 01364 654749

Brimblecombe's Cider
Farrants Farm, Dunsford, Exeter,
Devon, EX6 7BA
T: 01647 252783

Broadoak Cider
Blackberry Hill, Clutton, Somerset,
BS39 5QQ
T: 01275 333154

Gray's Devon Cider
Halstow, Tedburn St. Mary, Exeter,
Devon, EX6 6AN
T: 01647 61236

Green Valley Cyder
Darts Valley Farm, Clyst St George,
Devon, EX3 0QH
T: 01392 876658

Hecks Farmhouse Cider
9–11 Middle Leigh, Street, Somerset,
BA16 0LB
T: 01458 442367
www.hecksfarmhousecider.co.uk

George Perry of Perry's Cider, Somerset

Merrydown
2440 The Quadrant, Aztec West,
Almondsbury, Bristol, BS32 4AQ
T: 01454 878 703
www.merrydown.co.uk

Perry's Cider
Dowlish Wake, Ilminster, Somerset,
TA19 0NY
T: 01460 55195
www.perryscider.co.uk

Porthallow Vinyard
Porthallow Lane, St Keverne, Helston,
Cornwall, TR12 6QH
T: 01326 280050
www.cornwall-homepage.co.uk/
homepages/vinyard/index.html

Sheppy's Cider
Three Bridges, Bradford-on-Tone,
Taunton, Somerset, TA4 1ER
T: 01823 461233
www.sheppyscider.com

Thatchers
Myrtle Farm, Sandford, Somerset,
BS25 5RA
T: 01934 822862
www.thatcherscider.co.uk

Winkleigh Cider Co
Western Barn, Hatherleigh Road,
Winkleigh, Devon, EX19 8AP
T: 01837 83560
www.winkleighcider.co.uk

Yarde Cider
Broad Path, Stoke Gabriel, Devon,
TQ9 6RH
T: 01803 782217
www.realdrink.org

Kent, Sussex & Surrey

Biddenden
Biddenden Vineyards, Gribble Bridge
Lane, Biddenden, Kent, TN27 8DF
T: 01580 291726
www.biddendenvineyards.com

Coldharbour Cider
Leith Hill Place Lodge, Coldharbour,
Dorking, Surrey
T: 01306 712140

Double Vision Cidery
Marlpit Farm, Wierton Road,
Boughton Monchelsea, Maidstone,
Kent, ME17 4JW
T: 01622 746633

Gospel Green
Gospel Green Cottage, Haslemere,
Sussex, GU27 3BH
T: 01428 654120

Pawley Farm Cider
Painters Forstal, Ospringe, Kent,
ME13 0EN
T: 01795 532043

Sedlescombe Organic Vinyard
Cripps Corner, Robertsbridge,
East Sussex, TN32 5SA
T: 0800 980 2884
www.englishorganicwine.co.uk

East Anglia

Aspall
The Cyder House, Aspall Hall,
Debenham, Suffolk, IP14 6PD
T: 01728 860510
www.aspall.co.uk

Crones Organic Apple Juice and Cider
Fairview, Fersfield Rd, Kenninghall,
Norfolk, NR16 2DP
T: 01379 687687
www.crones.co.uk

Shawsgate Cider
Shawsgate Vineyard, Bodingham Road,
Framlingham, Suffolk, IP13 9HZ
T: 01728 724060

Nurseries

Cider apple and perry pear trees are rarely available from your local garden centre, but there are a number of specialist tree nurseries in the country where you can obtain traditional varieties. Some nurseries are able to fulfil specific orders like grafting your chosen variety onto a different rootstock if you have restricted growing space, most stock trees of various ages, and they should all be able to advise on the right trees for your plot of land – so if you're tempted to make your own single varietal ciders from your own apples then there's no excuse.

Adam's Apples
Egremont Barn, Payhembury,
Honiton, Devon, EX14 3JA
T: 01404 841166
www.talatonplants.co.uk

Agroforestry Research Trust
46 Hunters Moon, Dartington,
Totnes, Devon, TQ9 6JT
T: 01803 840776
www.agroforestry.co.uk

The Apple Factor
109 Woodmancote, Dursley,
Gloucestershire, GL11 4AH
T: 01453 545675
www.sarahjuniper.co.uk/applefactor

Bernwode Plants
Kingswood Lane, Ludgershall,
Buckinghamshire, HP18 9RB
T: 01844 237415
www.bernwodeplants.co.uk

Chris Bowers & Sons
Wimbotsham, Norfolk, PE34 3QB
T: 01366 388752
www.chrisbowers.co.uk

Brogdale Horticultural Trust
Brogdale Farm, Brogdale Road,
Faversham, Kent, ME13 8XZ
T: 01795 535286
www.brogdale.org

Buckingham Nurseries
Tingewick Road, Buckingham,
MK18 4AE
T: 01280 822133
www.buckingham-nurseries.co.uk

Butterworths' Organic Nursery
Garden Cottage, Auchinleck House
Estate, Cumnock, Ayrshire, KA18 2LR
T: 01290 551088
www.butterworthsorganicnursery.
co.uk

Crown Nursery
High Street, Ufford, Suffolk, IP13 6EL
T: 01394 460755
www.crown-nursery.co.uk

Deacon's Nursery
Moor View, Godshill, Isle of Wight,
PO38 3HW
T: 01983 840750
www.deaconsnurseryfruits.co.uk

Eden Point Nurseries
20 Giller Drive, Penwortham, Preston,
Lancashire, PR1 9LT
www.edenpointnurseries.co.uk

Keepers Nursery
Gallants Court, East Farleigh,
Maidstone, Kent, ME15 0LE
T: 01622 726465
www.fruittree.co.uk

Lodge Farm Trees
Lodge Farm, Rockhampton, Berkeley,
Gloucestershire, GL13 9DY
T: 01454 260310
www.lodgefarmtrees.co.uk

Ornamental Tree Nurseries
Cobnash, Kingsland, Herefordshire,
HR6 9QZ
T: 01568 708016
www.ornamental-trees.co.uk

Paul Jasper Trees
The Lighthouse, Bridge Street,
Leominster, Herefordshire, HR6 8DX
www.jaspertrees.co.uk

Thornhayes Nursery
St. Andrews Wood, Dulford,
Cullompton, EX15 2DF
T: 01884 266746
www.thornhayes-nursery.co.uk

Victoriana Nursery Gardens
Challock, Nr Ashford, Kent,
TN25 4DG
T: 01233 740529
www.victoriananursery.co.uk

Walcot Organic Nursery
Lower Walcot Farm, Walcot Lane,
Drakes Broughton, Pershore,
Worcestershire, WR10 2AL
T: 01905 841587
www.walcotnursery.co.uk

Index

Page numbers in *italic* refer to the illustrations

Books for Beer Lovers

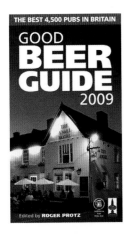

Good Beer Guide 2009

Editor: Roger Protz

The *Good Beer Guide* is the only guide you will ever need to find the right pint, in the right place, every time. Now in its 36th year, the *Good Beer Guide* is fully revised and updated, with information on more than 4,500 recommended pubs, including those which serve draught cider, and a unique section listing all the breweries – micro, regional and national – that produce cask beer in the UK.

£14.99 ISBN 978-1-85249-249-6

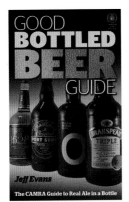

Good Bottled Beer Guide

Jeff Evans

A pocket-sized guide for discerning drinkers looking to buy bottled real ales and enjoy a fresh glass of their favourite beers at home. The 7th edition of the *Good Bottled Beer Guide* is completely revised, updated and redesigned to showcase the very best bottled British real ales now being produced, and detail where they can be bought. Everything you need to know about bottled beers; tasting notes, ingredients, brewery details, and a glossary to help the reader understand more about them.

£12.99 ISBN 978-1-85249-262-5

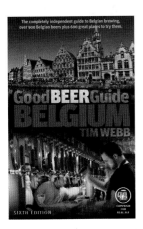

Good Beer Guide Belgium

Tim Webb

The completely revised and updated 6th edition of the guide so impressive that it is acknowledged as the standard work for Belgian beer lovers, even in Belgium itself. The *Good Beer Guide Belguim* includes comprehensive advice on getting there, being there, what to eat, where to stay and how to bring beers back home. Its outline of breweries, beers and bars makes this book indispensible for both leisure and business travellers a well as for armchair drinkers looking to enjoy a selection of Belgian brews from their local beer store.

£14.99 ISBN 978-1-85249-261-8

London Heritage Pubs – An inside story

Geoff Brandwood & Jane Jephcote

The definitive guidebook to London's most unspoilt pubs. Raging from gloriously rich Victorian extravaganzas to unspoilt community street-corner locals, the pubs not only have interiors of genuine heritage value, they also have fascinating stories to tell. *London Heritage Pubs — An inside story* is a must for anyone interested in visiting and learning about London's magnificent pubs.

£14.99   ISBN 978-1-85249-247-2

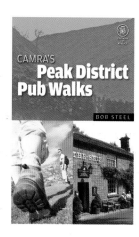

Peak District Pub Walks

Bob Steel

A practical, pocket-sized traveller's guide to some of the best pubs and best walking in the Peak District. This book features 25 walks, as well as cycle routes and local attractions, helping you see the best of Britain's oldest national park while never straying too far from a decent pint. Each route has been selected for its inspiring landscape, historical interest and welcoming pubs.

£9.99   ISBN 978-1-85249-246-5

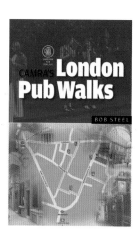

London Pub Walks

Bob Steel

A practical, pocket-sized guide enabling you to explore the English capital while never being far away from a decent pint. The book includes 30 walks around more than 180 pubs serving fine real ale, from the heart of the City and bustling West End to majestic riverside routes and the leafy Wimbledon Common. Each pub is selected for its high-quality real ale, its location and its superb architectural heritage. The walks feature more pubs than any other London pub-walk guide.

£8.99   ISBN 978-1-85249-216-8

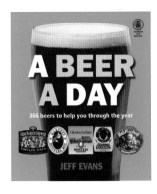

A Beer a Day
Jeff Evans

Written by leading beer writer Jeff Evans, *A Beer a Day* is a beer lover's almanac, crammed with beers from around the world to enjoy on every day and in every season, and celebrating beer's connections with history, sport, music film and television. Whether it's Christmas Eve, Midsummer's Day, Bonfire Night, or just a wet Wednesday in the middle of October, *A Beer a Day* has just the beer for you to savour and enjoy.

£16.99   **ISBN 978-1-85249-235-9**

100 Belgian Beers to Try Before You Die!
Tim Webb & Joris Pattyn

100 Belgian Beers to Try Before You Die! showcases 100 of the best Begian beers as chosen by internationally-known beer writers Tim Webb and Joris Pattyn. Lavishly illustrated throughout with images of the beers, breweries, Belgian beer bars and some of the characters involved in Belgian brewing, the book encourages both connoisseurs and newcomers to Belgian beer to sample them for themselves, both in Belgium and at home.

£12.99   **ISBN 987-1-85249-248-9**

300 Beers to Try Before You Die!
Roger Protz

300 beers from around the world, handpicked by award-winning journalist, author and broadcaster Roger Protz to try before you die! A comprehensive portfolio of top beers from the smallest microbreweries in the United States to family-run British breweries and the world's largest brands. This book is indispensible for both beer novices and aficionados.

£12.99   **ISBN 978-1-85249-213-7**

It takes all sorts to Campaign for Real Ale

CAMRA, the Campaign for Real Ale, is an independent not-for-profit,
volunteer-led consumer group. We promote good-quality real ale
and pubs as well as lobbying government to champion
drinkers' rights and protect local pubs as centres of community life.

CAMRA has 90,000 members from all ages and backgrounds,
brought together by a common belief in the issues that CAMRA
deals with and their love of good quality British beer and cider.
From just £20 a year – that's less than a pint a month – you can join
CAMRA and enjoy the following benefits:

A monthly colour newspaper informing you about beer and pub news
and detailing events and beer festivals around the country.

Free or reduced entry to over 140 national, regional and local beer festivals.

Money off many of our publications including the
Good Beer Guide and the *Good Bottled Beer Guide*.

Access to a members-only section of our national website,
www.camra.org.uk, which gives up-to-the-minute news stories
and includes a special offer section with regular features
saving money on beer and trips away.

The opportunity to campaign to save pubs under threat
of closure, for pubs to be open when people want to drink and a
reduction in beer duty that will help Britain's brewing industry survive.

Log onto **www.camra.org.uk** for
CAMRA membership information.

**CAMPAIGN
FOR
REAL ALE**

Do you feel passionately about your pint? Then why not join CAMRA

Just fill in the application form (or a photocopy of it) and the Direct Debit form on the next page to receive three months' membership FREE!*

If you wish to join but do not want to pay by Direct Debit, please fill in the application form below and send a cheque, payable to **CAMRA**, to: CAMRA, 230 Hatfield Road, St Albans, Hertfordshire, AL1 4LW. Please note than non Direct Debit payments will incur a £2 surcharge. Figures are given below.

Please tick appropriate box

	Direct Debit		Non Direct Debit	
Single membership (UK & EU)	£20	☐	£22	☐
Concessionary membership (under 26 or 60 and over)	£14	☐	£16	☐
Joint membership	£25	☐	£27	☐
Concessionary joint membership	£17	☐	£19	☐

Life membership information is available on request.

Title _____ Surname _____

Forename(s)_____

Address_____

_____ Postcode _____

Date of Birth _____ Email address _____

Signature _____

Partner's details (for Joint Membership)

Title _____ Surname _____

Forename(s)_____

Date of Birth _____ Email address _____

CAMRA will occasionally send you e-mails related to your membership. We will also allow your local branch access to your email. If you would like to opt-out of contact from your local branch please tick here ☐ (at no point will your details be released to a third party).

Find out more about CAMRA at **www.camra.org.uk**   Telephone 01727 867201

*Three months free is only available the first time a member pays by DD

CAMPAIGN FOR REAL ALE

Instruction to your Bank or Building Society to pay by Direct Debit

⬤ DIRECT Debit

Please fill in the form and send to: Campaign for Real Ale Ltd. 230 Hatfield Road, St. Albans, Herts. AL1 4LW

Name and full postal address of your Bank or Building Society

To The Manager _____ Bank or Building Society

Address _____

_____

Postcode _____

Name (s) of Account Holder (s)

_____

Bank or Building Society account number

Branch Sort Code

Reference Number

Banks and Building Societies may not accept Direct Debit Instructions for some types of account

Originator's Identification Number

9	2	6	1	2	9

FOR CAMRA OFFICIAL USE ONLY
This is not part of the instruction to your **Bank or Building Society**

Membership Number _____

Name _____

Postcode _____

Instruction to your Bank or Building Society

Please pay CAMRA Direct Debits from the account detailed on this Instruction subject to the safeguards assured by the Direct Debit Guarantee. I understand that this instruction may remain with CAMRA and, if so, will be passed electronically to my Bank/Building Society

Signature(s) _____

Date _____

✂ detached and retained this section

This Guarantee should be detached and retained by the payer.

⬤ DIRECT Debit

The Direct Debit Guarantee

- This Guarantee is offered by all Banks and Building Societies that take part in the Direct Debit Scheme. The efficiency and security of the Scheme is monitored and protected by your own Bank or Building Society.

- If the amounts to be paid or the payment dates change CAMRA will notify you 10 working days in advance of your account being debited or as otherwise agreed.

- If an error is made by CAMRA or your Bank or Building Society, you are guaranteed a full and immediate refund from your branch of the amount paid.

- You can cancel a Direct Debit at any time by writing to your Bank or Building Society. Please also send a copy of your letter to us.